POE'S CHILDREN

PETER LANG
New York • Washington, D.C./Baltimore • Boston • Bern
Frankfurt am Main • Berlin • Brussels • Vienna • Canterbury

Tony Magistrale and Sidney Poger

POE'S CHILDREN

Connections between Tales
of Terror and Detection

PETER LANG
New York • Washington, D.C./Baltimore • Boston • Bern
Frankfurt am Main • Berlin • Brussels • Vienna • Canterbury

Library of Congress Cataloging-in-Publication Data

Magistrale, Tony.
Poe's children: connections between tales
of terror and detection / Tony Magistrale and Sidney Poger.
p. cm.
Includes bibliographical references and index.
1. Detective and mystery stories, American—History and criticism.
2. Detective and mystery stories, English—History and criticism. 3. Horror tales,
American—History and criticism. 4. Horror tales, English—History and criticism.
5. Motion picture plays—History and criticism. 6. Poe, Edgar Allan, 1809–1849—Influence.
7. English fiction—American influences. 8. Gothic revival
(Literature). 9. Literary form. I. Poger, Sidney. II. Title.
PS374.D4M26   813'.087209—dc21   98-53779
ISBN 0-8204-4070-1

Die Deutsche Bibliothek-CIP-Einheitsaufnahme

Magistrale, Tony:
Poe's children: connections between tales
of terror and detection / Tony Magistrale and Sidney Poger.
–New York; Washington, D.C./Baltimore; Boston; Bern;
Frankfurt am Main; Berlin; Brussels; Vienna; Canterbury: Lang.
ISBN 0-8204-4070-1

Cover design by Nona Rueter

The paper in this book meets the guidelines for permanence and durability
of the Committee on Production Guidelines for Book Longevity
of the Council of Library Resources.

∞

Printed in the United States of America

To Ruth Poger, Jennifer Magistrale, and
the University of Vermont students of "Poe's Children,"
we gratefully dedicate this book.

About the Cover Artist

Lynn Barnes began drawing at age one and a half and started painting in oils at age 14. She graduated from the University of Maryland, Baltimore County, with a bachelor's degree in the Visual and Performing Arts with an emphasis on Art. Since then she has studied German Language and Literature and attended the classical Schuler School of Fine Arts, where they teach anatomy and the chemistry of painting. She grinds her own pigments. Her paintings are inspired by music, literature, history, and mysticism and can take up to 1,500 hours to complete. She lives in a historic house in Fells Point, Baltimore, which she shares with Hieronymus, her African Gray Parrot.

Poe's Last Supper

Edgar Allan Poe died on 7 October 1849 on the third floor of what is now Church Home Hospital in Baltimore. He was only 40 years old. Doctors have hypothesized that he died of everything from alcohol poisoning, diabetes, to rabies. One thing we do know, he hallucinated. Now what would Poe hallucinate, especially on his deathbed?

In the painting, depicted on the cover, Poe is propped up in a hospital bed, but he thinks he is in a Fells Point bar drinking absinthe and eating oysters with his characters. They are counter-clockwise from the upper left:

Ligea *struggles with* The Conqueror Worm, The Raven *stands on* The Cask of Amontillado, Hop-Frog *the dwarf strokes* The Black Cat. *To the right of Poe, sitting beside the executioner at the table is the Grand Inquisitor* (The Pit and the Pendulum). *The figure of the Inquisitor is derived from a portrait of Rufus Griswold, Poe's real-life arch enemy and literary executor. He is offering Poe a notice of an "Auto de Fe" (in English an "Act of Faith") which is an interesting thing to call a public torture display. It is also interesting, even unimaginable, that the Spanish Inquisition slowly ground to a halt during Poe's lifetime. Its real end came on 6 June 1869 when the principle of religious tolerance became a part of the Spanish constitution. It had an over 700-year history. To the right of Griswold, a couple of glasses and a* Gold Bug *are taken away by an orderly/bartender with a very loud heart only Poe can hear. Behind him,* Arthur Gordon Pym *holds a large sea turtle which will help him stay alive after a shipwreck. The turtle has water stored in the back of its head. Jupiter (with the Scythe) and Captain Kidd (thank you Steve Bunker) from* The Gold Bug *watch Ligea's struggle with the worms. An Indian stands guard from* The Ragged Mountains. *In July 1849, Poe spent some time in a cell at Moyanesing prison in Philadelphia, supposedly for drunkenness. Upon his release, Poe sought his friend, a cockney publisher and engraver named John Sartain, who also lived in Philadelphia who would publish posthumously Poe's last work* The Bells. *Poe was still hallucinating when he told Sartain of his vision in prison of the Silver Lady. Poe was convinced she tried to trick him with questions in the hope she could snare him for death. In the painting she symbolically rings the last of* The Bells, *the death bell. She is the only non-literary figure present.*

Through the window, a small ship, The Annabel Lee *is moored on the rocks beneath the Cape Hatteras lighthouse from* The Oblong Box.

The painting has been worked on over a period of six years. Since its inception, several friends of mine that have spent many years researching Poe's life and works said some of the nurses did overhear Poe talk to some of the characters on his deathbed. Imagine that.

Lynn Barnes
August 1998

Acknowledgments

The authors wish to acknowledge several individuals and institutions who helped to make this book a reality. First, and perhaps most important, the University of Vermont student alumni from English 184: "Poe's Children," for their unflagging interest in the material and their contributions that helped to shape the contents of this book. In addition, our editor at Peter Lang, Heidi Burns, supplied sound advice and encouragement all along the way. To Dawn Pelkey for her patience and contributions to the debate the authors posed on material in and out of class. To the University of Vermont for sabbatical time for both authors to compose this volume. And to the Dean's Fund of the College of Arts and Sciences for financial support. A portion of Chapter 1 was initially published in the magazine *Gadfly* while a version of Chapter 2 appeared originally in *Clues: A Journal of Detection.* The authors wish to acknowledge and thank these two publications.

Contents

Introduction 1

Chapter 1. Originating Lines: The Importance of Poe 11

Chapter 2. Poe's Children: The Conjunction of the
Detective and Gothic Tales 29

Chapter 3. Poe's Victorian Disguises:
The Hound of the Baskervilles and *Dr. Jekyll and Mr. Hyde* 45

Chapter 4. Poe Feminized: Daughters of Fear and Detection 57

Chapter 5. Proportioning Poe: The Blurring of Horror
and Detection in *The Silence of the Lambs* 77

Chapter 6: The Overlook Hotel and Beyond:
Stephen King as Poe's Postmodern Heir 93

Chapter 7. Celluloid Poe: Detective *Noir* Meets
Hollywood Gothic... 113

Works Cited 131

Index 143

Introduction

A few years ago one of us was teaching a course in Detective Fiction, the other a class on Stephen King and the American Gothic Tradition. While we were brought together to collaborate on another unrelated writing project, we found ourselves returning to discussions on Poe and his influence on these two particular genres. We became excited with what we were discovering about our own special areas of scholarship by broadening our understanding of Poe. A year or so later, we decided to explore more formally these connections in a course at the University of Vermont called "Poe's Children," in which we shared lectures and narrative texts, students, and the insights they taught us. The course grew into the book you now have in your hands.

There is perhaps no other American writer, with the notable exception of Mark Twain, who manages to bridge the gap between popular culture and high-brow Literature to the degree that we have come to associate with Poe. He stands simultaneously as a figure at the center of Modernism—the line that stretches from Baudelaire and the Symbolist movement to T.S. Eliot and the rise of New Criticism—and as the inventor or innovator of several popular genres, including science fiction, and the two we will be tracing in this book: detective literature and Gothic horror. Poe continues to attract a large "non-literary" following, to the point where he has arguably distinguished himself as the most recognizable figure in the entire canon of American literature. His melancholic physiognomy is immediately recognizable when it stares out from tee-shirts and poster art available at suburban malls, while a raven perched in a tree or standing alongside the road inspires many of us to think of Poe and his most famous poem. He seems to be the one member of the American literati whose name is recognized, even by people who do not consider themselves serious readers. (As we will further elaborate in Chapter 6, Stephen King appears to be accomplishing a similar feat, but King is, after all, our contemporary, and his cultural longevity must ultimately be decided by future generations.) Poe's poem "The Raven" is still a favorite among school children forced to memorize a poem for class recitation, and it has now been immortalized in an unforgettable episode of *The Simpsons*.

All this popular attention must now be viewed, in part, as highly ironic. During his lifetime Poe knew mostly poverty and achieved only a modicum of the literary fame that he so resented in writers such as Longfellow and the Concord transcendentalists, whom Poe derisively labelled the "Frogpondians." Had it not been for the French, Poe might still be ignored or relegated to the slanderous and scurrilous character assassination rendered by his first biographer, Rufus Griswold, who insisted that Poe was a drug addict, sexually immoral, and that every one of Poe's depraved, homicidal, or suicidal characters were personal portraits. At any rate, Poe's reputation and art were first rescued by a European audience, who thankfully alerted Americans (and the rest of the world) to what they were missing.

Indeed, Poe's path differs from those of the other American writers of his time, deviating from the unflagging (and untiring) optimism of the transcendentalists, as well as from the darker, more didactic writings of Hawthorne and Melville. Poe is the American Shakespeare of the lunatic asylum, exploring a compressed world populated by psyches out of control. His theoretic insistence on the primacy of shorter work is perfectly suited to the wandering attention span of a modern reader, while his fascination with human disaster is treated either comically (in the satires and burlesques) or taken to the extreme of seriousness in his elaborate studies of psychopathology.

Poe's Gothic tales reveal the human propensity for self-destruction, for doing those things which are neither healthy nor socially acceptable, what Poe called "the perverse." Poe documented the irrational power of perversity to govern human life. In the obsessional voices of his overwrought narrators, the reader gradually becomes aware that their madness supersedes their acts of criminality. This energy is released through Poe's employment of the Gothic, in the murder in "The Tell-Tale Heart" or the oral fixation of the narrator in "Berenice." His detective tales, on the other hand, acknowledge that same energy, but here Poe labors to contain it through the efforts of the detective. Violent animal instincts, whether they belong to the human beast or to the ourang-outang in "The Murders in the Rue Morgue," are comprehensible to the mind of Dupin, and ultimately controllable in its capture and containment. The detective inhabits a world controlled by his mind, in which the inexplicable can be balanced and explained. The evolution of the detective story presents a world, no matter how mean, into which the detective brings order and rationality. Through his narratological presentations of these two apparent extremes, rationality and terror, Poe brought the two sides of his mind together.

Genre Archetypes and Paradigms

In utilizing Gothic themes and paraphernalia, Poe embellished and advanced an already established tradition. But he actually invented the detective story, although not out of whole cloth. Edmund Wilson, in "Who Cares Who Killed Roger Ackroyd," criticizes the detective tale as failing as literature, not possessing the style and artistic substance of our greatest and most enduring writing. But we discover the roots of detective fiction as early as classical Greek drama. *Oedipus Rex* can be read as a tale of a detective committed to finding the murderer of King Lauis and relieving

Thebes from the plague that cursed it. In his search to uncover the murderer, Oedipus interviews a number of people: Teiresias, Creon, Jocasta, the shepherd, and the messenger from Corinth. As he draws closer to the goal of his search, he is given a "false clue" by Jocasta, that her first husband was killed by marauders at a crossroads. Oedipus, like any good detective, eventually solves the crime and punishes the perpetrator; since he himself is the murderer, he puts out his own eyes in acknowledgment of his guilt.

A second early detective story is that of Shakespeare's *Hamlet*, whose play-within-a-play is more proof of guilt than an attempt to uncover who has committed the crime. His father's ghost tells Hamlet of its own murder, being overtaken in sleep in the garden; his brother Claudius poured poison in his ear. Hamlet does not like his uncle, but he cannot proceed without proof. So he uses the visiting players to provide a metatextual play about a murder that parallels his father's death. Claudius is so upset by the performance that Hamlet is satisfied with the proof and goes on to seek revenge.

And yet a third example of an ancient detective tale is that of Susanna and the Elders from the Bible. The Elders, lusting after Susanna, are refused by her and, to punish her, they accuse her of adultery with a young man whom they could not capture. As she is being led away to be stoned, Daniel stops the procedure and calls the party back to the place of judgment. There he questions the Elders separately, asking each under what kind of tree they captured Susanna. Each answers a different tree, and because their answers do not concur, they are condemned out of their own mouths. In the tradition of justice prevailing, or the concept of ethical enthusiasm often used in discussions of detective fiction, the Elders are stoned in Susanna's place.

Perhaps one of our earliest exposures to the narrative of detection, although seldom appreciated as such because it is also a famous fairy tale, is "Goldilocks and the Three Bears." It contains to some degree all the major elements of the detective story. While the three bears walk in the forest to allow their porridge to cool, having left their front door ajar, Goldilocks comes along and commits a crime: technically, entering (as no breaking is involved) or trespassing. She proceeds, first, to eat the baby bear's porridge (a theft of property), second, to break the baby bear's chair (malicious destruction of property), and, third, to fall asleep upstairs in the baby bear's bed. The bears, our detectives in this tale, put together clues in a rational manner: "Someone's been eating my porridge," etc. Their method of questioning builds up suspense; after all, they follow the same formula nine times. The bear family discovers the culprit when they come upon Goldilocks asleep. While it may appear that Goldilocks escapes without punishment, her fright at being awakened by three bears surely presents dramatic consequences for her multiple crimes. Moreover, she jumps out the back window—the bears' house must have been built on the side of a hill for her to avoid injury—and runs home, learning never to wander in the forest alone again, as well as not to enter the homes of strangers. A crime has been committed, the detectives detect, and the perpetrator is eventually discovered and punished.

The roots of horror art go back at least as far as the examples we have cited as early archetypes of detection. Certainly the revelatory moment that Oedipus experiences when he learns that he himself is the monster who has killed his father and slept with his mother is about as terrifying an experience as any to be found in the horror genre. And the blood and gore that soak the stage in Act 5 of *Hamlet* are as plentiful as any to be found in a contemporary slasher film. In both horror and detection individuals and the human community itself are threatened by a destructive agency. In the horror tale, heroic members of the community come together to vanquish evil and restore the security of their community, as in Stephen King's *IT*. This is exactly the same narrative pattern found in English detective novels from what is called the Golden Age of Detection. A peaceful, restricted society is disrupted by some perpetrator of serious crime. To counterbalance its influence, reason and ratiocination are employed to discover the identity of the murderer. The murderer is then banished, and order is restored.

This is the classic paradigm for both horror and detection. But sometimes these conventional notions are undermined, particularly in *film noir* detective texts and contemporary horror art. The best works of horror and detection often suggest a certain level of ambiguity in the struggle between good and evil. Even Poe's C. Auguste Dupin, the first literary detective, should not be characterized as an essentially moral being; he solves crimes less for society's welfare than his own. Dupin is a recluse who takes refuge in the exotic realm of his imagination wherein he is able to identify with the criminal mind. Not only do moral polarities seem difficult to sustain underneath the surface of all things human, but conclusions themselves are not always easily resolved by the triumph of good.

The Gothic has always invited its audience to acknowledge, and fear, the shadow that dwells within. The premise that underscores the Gothic's obsessional reliance upon the psychology of the double is that we ought to be afraid — and of nothing so much as ourselves (Edmundson 11). Detection stories seek to resolve the moral chaos put into motion by a particular criminal act. But in films such as *Chinatown, Blade Runner*, and *Seven*, for example, the detective loses his sense of purposefulness and gets an intimate glimpse into the ambiguity of the horror monster. In the end, the full range of narratological alternatives in both Gothic horror and detection do less to subvert genre archetypes and narrative paradigms than to suggest their mutual possibilities for the production of serious art.

Connecting Genres

It is the mating of terror and detection that we celebrate in this book. Since both spring from the same impulse, they have many concerns in common. The central thesis points that unify this book are examined, to greater or lesser extents, in each of the forthcoming chapters, but especially in Chapter 2. By way of an introductory encapsulation, then, the Gothic can be seen to intersect the detective story in the following ways:

1. Each genre begins with a peaceful state; i.e., a period before the murder is committed, the evil unleashed, or the supernatural animated.

2. The actions of the monster/criminal are the forces that animate the plots of the horror/crime story. Oftentimes, the identities of both are not immediately revealed, but eventually the audience must learn the cause of the chaos and the perpetrator's identity.

3. The audience's interest in the monster/criminal increases during the course of the narrative. We want to know more about these beings: their motivations, purposes, powers, and personalities, and even their potential flaws which may aid in their capture or destruction. Monsters and murderers live outside the realms of order and restraint; they are the Other, the ambiguous embodiments of our bipolar fear of chaos and the urge towards absolute freedom.

4. Both the monster and the murderer must eventually be confronted. The disclosures of the horrific being and criminal represent core elements of narrative in both genres; even after the identity of the creature/criminal is known, the audience remains focused upon whether such a confrontation will vanquish the perpetrator of evil.

5. The detective is at the center of the crime narrative, frequently serving as its storyteller. The Gothic tale likewise often features a hero(ine), but s/he exercises less control over events than does the detective. Perhaps this is so because the detective archetype relies upon the logic of deductive analysis to solve the crime while the horror tale is less logically demarcated. The detective also maintains a certain critical distance in the narrative; characters such as Dupin and Sherlock Holmes stand both within and without, a part of the action, yet somehow above it. The horror protagonist, in contrast, is never very far removed from the fray; Dr. Jekyll, for example, is intimately immersed in the circumstances that cause him to experience terror. It is the detective Utterson that stands apart from the action. Thus, the

tragic possibilities of horror art, including the deeply personal suffering that often occurs, are seldom paralleled in detective fiction.

6. In order to assemble information to solve the crime, the detective narrative focuses upon events that have already occurred. The horror genre, to create and maintain a higher level of tension and terror, is more apt to center on events taking place in the present.

7. The two genres both seek revelation: detection via the revelation of the criminal, horror art via the destruction of the monster. The Gothic often includes a certain level of transcendence that occurs as a consequence of the confrontation with evil: heroic characters pay terrible emotional and psychic costs for the opportunity to change, mature, and evolve morally. If they survive, many horror hero(ines) do so as scarred beings who resemble little of their former selves. But this is not always such a terrible thing. As Stephen King suggests in *Danse Macabre*, terror "arises from a pervasive sense of disestablishment, that things are in the unmaking," which must be followed by some type of reconfiguration or remaking (22). This deeply personal struggle sometimes occurs in the detective tale, particularly as we have noted in *film noir* detection, but more generally the detective represents a fixed moral point, remaining a constant personality throughout the text.

8. Both genres strive to end with a restitution of the norm: the monster is dispatched, the hero(ine) survives; once the criminal is caught, the detective's job is finished, and s/he moves on to another case. Each genre teaches us something about the consequences of moral transgression and the violation of social taboo.

The expression of horror or murder, the discovery of the source of that disturbing influence, the attempts to deal with it through moral struggle, false clues, or the overcoming of evil forces, and the conclusion —either in identification of the murderer or the source of horror—bring these two genres together. As in Poe, it is the discovery or dramatization of evil which is uppermost in the mind of both author and reader, the accessing of knowledge which is also the power to fend off evil.

How to Use This Book

This book should prove useful in reading Poe. In interpreting several of his most significant works of fiction and non-fiction, its authors are concerned with providing a specific exegesis of Poe's views on terror and detection. In the process, our readings will reveal Poe's most significant (and contradictory) contributions to literature: the urge toward self-destruction, self-transcendence, and self-knowledge. This understanding will then be extended to other writers who follow Poe in time and temperament so that Poe's work comes to represent not only his own accomplishments, but a portion of theirs as well.

We have also composed a genre study, defining both horror and detective tales from their primal fascination with the irrationalities of life to recognizing the basis of this irrationality in the repressed unconsciousness of the individual and in the forces of cultural oppression. Readers of the horror story will explore the bifurcated attraction-repulsion response they have to the telling of a good horror tale. The audience of the detective story will recognize the impulse toward ethical enthusiasm which dominates the form and which colors the expectations of readers to have everything resolved at the conclusion of the narrative.

The book also can be read as a study of individual detective and horror tales, ranging over a series of important authors, to deepen the meanings of their art. Individual chapters contextualize writers within two distinct but nonetheless related traditions, so that the permutations of the Gothic can be seen operating in an archetypical detective narrative, and vice versa. Thus, our text's unique emphasis is upon the ghostliness of *The Hound of the Baskervilles*, the rationality of *Dr. Jekyll and Mr. Hyde*, and the complete blurring of genre definitions in Thomas Harris's *The Silence of the Lambs*.

Poe's Children will prove useful in interpreting writers and filmmakers who follow Poe, especially in those who, more or less, combine the two traditions of detective and horror art. *Dr. Jekyll and Mr. Hyde* deepens its emotional content from the desperate attempt to apply the rationality of detection to the growing world of horror; likewise, *The Hound of the Baskervilles*, proceeds from the supernatural dimensions of the tale of detection, leading to an acknowledgment of the power of the irrational, even in the world of the rational. The female writers who have been influenced by Poe show another dimension, the extension of horror and detection into once-tabooed domains controlled almost exclusively by male writers. These women authors take their subtle revenge, drawing characters who evolve from victim status to avenging agents, thereby transforming the horror and detective genres and their timeless propensity for exploiting women. It is in our treatment of *The Silence of the Lambs* where the thesis of this book is perhaps most fully realized, as Harris's novel is at once both a tale of psychological terror and a study in rationality as a means for the detective to contain and survive its onslaught. The chapter on Stephen King concludes that Poe is an important shaping influence upon arguably the most popular and influential writer in the world today. It postulates that these two writers share common ground that extends even beyond their mutual Gothic inheritance.

This book's final chapter, dealing with Poe and film, discusses the influence of Poe—direct as well as indirect—on contemporary cinema. Some readers may be puzzled about the absence of director Alfred Hitchcock from this chapter's discussion, as Hitchcock has acknowledged his debt to Poe in several interviews. Certainly the haunted house and chilling landscape of *Psycho* and the infernal doublings of *Vertigo* suggest the profound impressions that "The Fall of the House of Usher" and "Ligeia" created upon the imagination of the director. But while Hitchcock's canon relies heavily upon Gothic influences in both at-mosphere and psychology, there are really no most important detectives in his films, except for in *Psycho* and *Rear Window*. In *Psycho* the detective is dispatched rather quickly; in *Rear Window* he is called upon to help in the investigation, but he only gets in the way. His main function is to rescue the photographer at the end of the film and arrest the murderer. It might be argued, on the other hand, that many of Hitchcock's male protagonists operate in a way that at least suggests the detective genre insofar as they are all trying to solve a problem by unravelling a mystery. As Robin Wood has noted in *Hitchcock's Films*, "The Hitchcock hero typically lives in a small, enclosed world of his own fabrication, at once a protection and a prison, artificial and unrealistic, into which the 'real' chaos erupts, demanding to be faced" (69). But as most of these Hitchcock heroes, often played by Jimmy Stewart, find themselves cast suddenly into unaccustomed roles (e.g., a photographer as witness to a murder in *Rear Window*), their response is quite different from that of the conventional detective, and thus the horror of the situation is dramatically increased as a result of their participation rather than alleviated.

Chapter 7 begins with Roger Corman's series of films directed in the early 1960s based on Poe stories (or, at least on Poe titles). Unfortunately, in the process of creating nearly a film a year on a tight budget for a drive-in generation of teenage consumers, Poe's literary subtleties are often blunted in Corman's evocation of visual terror and physical catastrophe. Perhaps as a consequence of these limitations, Corman's attraction to Poe, while well known for many years, has been generally unappreciated by film critics and Poe scholars alike; it is certainly time for a Corman retrospective, and we can only hope that our discussion of his films will encourage other scholars and filmgoers alike to take up his cause. The other films detailed in this final chapter—*Chinatown, Seven*, and *Blade Runner*—essentially encapsulate the central thesis of this book, combining, in varying degrees, the rationality of detection with the freneticism of horror.

In the end, *Poe's Children* is an attempt to appreciate both the art of Edgar Allan Poe and his inimitable influence upon generations of writers and film directors who have read him. This influence is so vast, however, that a book like ours must necessarily limit itself to a few outstanding continental representations. Indeed, because we have deliberately restricted discussion to horror and detection in American and British artists, we were forced to exclude Poe's children from other cultures, most notably Europe and Latin America. Another book, similar in purpose to this one, will someday need to be written that traces Poe's lineage from Franz Kafka to Jorge Luis Borges. Then another that focuses upon Poe's musical progeny, from Claude Debussy's operas based upon two of Poe's stories to the Alan Parsons Project's instrumental renditions of electronically simulated voices that recite various lines and passages from Poe's poetry and tales. And perhaps one more book that will attempt to define the shape of the writer's influence in visual form, from Vincent Van Gogh, who had read broadly in Poe, and the *Art Nouveau* painters of the last third of the nineteenth century to the macabre and often grotesque cartoon worlds of Charles Addams and Gahan Wilson. Edgar Allan Poe never produced any biological offspring during his lifetime, but clearly his literary children are everywhere.

Chapter 1
Originating Lines: The Importance of Poe

Poe's was a master's vision of the terror that stalks about and within us, and the worm that writhes and slavers in the hideously close abyss. (Lovecraft 54)

[Poe] is the undisputed father of the detective story, although he would be disconcerted by many of his children and grandchildren. (Symons 35)

Romanticism is untidy and imprecise. The concept is almost as difficult to define as are the precise dates of its history. And certainly its evolution, extending from the Gothic revolution of the late eighteenth century to the middle of the nineteenth century, was in part a reaction against the rational objectivity of eighteenth-century Neoclassicism. While the neoclassical mind believed in an intelligible world maintained by a solid adherence to accepted tradition and form, the Romantic looked inward toward the self as the place where Truth and Beauty resided, and these were necessarily peculiar and private discoveries. It was an art of inner feeling, leading in turn to a yearning for the infinite. Because it was attracted to subjectivity and the unconscious, mystery, and the imagination, the Romantic sensibility tended to embrace the contradictions and complications of human nature. Since the Romantic artist was interested in blurring the boundaries separating the natural and the supernatural, the fantastic art that emerged was often about the unstable boundaries between what is real and what is illusion, what is lying and what is truth, what is normal and what is monstrous, what is hidden and what is revealed. Thus, under the Romantic rubric we find work that, on the one hand, embodies spiritual tranquility and inner poetic beauty while, on the other, the movement also contained elements of distortion and restlessness, a tortured awareness that the quest for tranquility and beauty was ultimately futile or perhaps forever lost.

It is helpful to keep these contradictions and dualisms in mind when considering Edgar Allan Poe as a quintessential Romantic writer, for, as he often yearned to dwell in an ideal sphere, particularly in his poetry, he also understood that untainted by dream or drug the world we normally inhabit was a decidedly unpoetic one. Even as he was passionately devoted to the Beautiful, he also knew that humankind was not. Poe embodied these two sides of a split Romantic legacy. His poetry, for example, often dreams of release into an Eden of the imagination. In "The Poetic Principle," he argues that poetry exalts the soul, transports us to a visionary realm, and that what we find most pleasurable about it is based on our human instinct for the beautiful. But for Poe, beauty was always connected to the "indefinite, pleasurable sadness" of all poetic themes—love, and, preferably, a lost or dead love. Thus, even as Poe, like Keats whom he profoundly admired, claimed poetry as a vehicle for transcendence to a better place, in many of his poems this quest is frequently interrupted, leaving the poet-narrator in a state of even greater spiritual torment.

When we turn to Poe's fiction, and especially his tales of terror and detection, it is not merely the sadness of lost love or the abrupt transition from or to a visionary landscape that inspires his deepest contemplation, but the complex spectrum of aberrant psychological motivation—ranging from sadomasochistic representations and object fixations to delusions of grandeur and the perversity of self-loathing. Throughout Poe's poetry and prose we find a Baconian aesthetic of a lovely distorted strangeness—lovely because it is distorted—that must incorporate the bizarre and the charnel in order to rank as beautiful. No one understood better than Poe that the deepest psychological truth may be rendered only through phantasmagoria.

But the phantasmagoria is not limited only to Poe's dream of the bizarre and the beautiful. It is also demonstrated in his use of the detective story, whose dream is of a mystery overcome by the mind of his detective, C. Auguste Dupin. While Poe's detective story comes from the same impulse toward romantic agony and its connection to the beautiful, it tries to meet it with the rational mind still left working from the Neoclassical period. But for the detective, as well as for the child of the Enlightenment, the rational mind is powerful enough to overcome the chaos inherent in human life. If the mystery has a life of its own, it can at least be confronted by the great amateur and tamed, if only for the moment. It is this impulse toward rationality which distinguishes the horror from the detective form, but their mutual reliance on mystery and the bizarre indicate the same root from which they sprung.

From the eighteenth century, Poe inherited both the Neoclassical impulse toward reason and rationality (as seen in his creation of the detective tale) and, conversely, the Gothic repudiation of a rational and ordered universe by dark, phantasmagorical forces beyond our ability to control (as dramatized in his tales of terror). As these two orientations would appear in opposition to one another, let us examine them separately, beginning with Poe's Gothic inheritance and, later in this chapter, turn to his adaptation of the Neoclassical mind in the formulation of the detective.

In his *Preface to the Second Edition of The Lyrical Ballads* (1800), Wordsworth railed against the "frantic novels" that appealed to a popular audience's "degrading thirst after outrageous stimulation" (455). His complaint failed to appreciate that the despised Gothic novel, which emerged as a dominant literary form in the last two decades of the eighteenth century, was simply the furthest extension of Wordsworth's own "spontaneous overflow of powerful feelings" (9). As Frederick Frank has pointed out, the Gothic phenomenon was an extreme manifestation of this overflow, since its "powerful feelings" were often sexual or psychopathic, but seldom "recollected in tranquility" (Frank 29).

By the time Poe begins writing seriously in the 1830s, the Gothic form was half a century old, supposedly obsolete, and the subject of numerous literary parodies and ridiculous examples of excess. But one of the most distinguishing features of the Gothic has always been its resiliency; the genre never did experience a final spasm and death. Instead, its original emphases on sentimental feeling, psychologically warped villains, chaste maidens, macabre settings, and supernatural occurrences were reconfigured and adapted for Romantic poems and Victorian novels throughout the nineteenth century. Poe, of course, had drunk deeply from the polluted waters of the Gothic well. The supernatural terror of Horace Walpole's first Gothic novel, *The Castle of Otranto* (1764), was an inspirational model for Poe's tale "Metzengerstein" and certain events, particularly the collapse of the mansion in "The Fall of the House of Usher," are modeled on the climax of Walpole's work. Similarly, it is probable that Poe found partial inspiration for many of his exotic settings and themes from his reading of William Beckford's *Vathek* (1786). This novel is mentioned in several of Poe's works including "The Premature Burial," *Pinakidia*, and "Thou Art the Man." And although he is named after Shakespeare's godlike creator of his own private world in *The Tempest*, Prospero in "The Masque of the Red Death" also closely resembles Beckford's sensuous and selfish caliph, Vathek, in his decadent behavior, lavish indulgences, and proud seclusion from the suffering masses of humanity. Likewise, Poe was fond of reciting Lord George Byron's poetry during his public recitations. The influence of the Byronic hero and attitudes on Poe's canon can be documented in letters, poems, and several tales. Many of Poe's characters, including Roderick Usher and C. Auguste Dupin, are direct transcriptions of the Byronic physiognomy and personality. That Poe was also familiar with vampire lore can be clearly substantiated in tales such as "Berenice," "Ligeia," and "Morella."

But in addition to recycling the Gothic paraphernalia of haunted mansions, mysterious ghosts and vampires, and psychosexually obsessed males, how did Poe reconfigure the Gothic for his own purposes? In other words, how did Poe actually advance the form by pushing horror to a higher plane?

When the Gothic crossed to American shores in the hands of Poe, it took on a particular psychological, cerebral slant. As Benjamin Franklin Fisher has generalized in his essay "The Residual Gothic Impulse: 1824–

1873": "There was a shift from physical fright, expressed through numerous outward miseries and villainous actions to psychological fear. The inward turn in fiction emphasized motivations, not their overt terrifying consequences" (177). This summation is perhaps best illustrated by the fact that very little action takes place in the typical Poe horror tale; the real energies in a story such as "The Imp of the Perverse," "The Man of the Crowd," or "The Tell-Tale Heart" are mental: the self tearing at the self. By depicting unstable minds unable to discipline their darkest urges, Poe's horror tales thrust even the reluctant reader inside the demented psyches of his characters. James B. Twitchell claims that Poe's art was the first to make the teller of the tale into an invading monster. We now have the Gothic story, not from the victim's point of view but from the victimizer's (46). Such a significant shift in narrative perspective forces the reader into an uncomfortable intimacy with the characters that is analogous to the role occupied by the viewer of the modern horror film. Like the horror film, Poe's tales produce contradictory tensions: the desire to watch and participate in unspeakable acts versus the wish to be free from monstrous drives. Aided by his propensity to employ first-person narration, Poe was the first writer to press the relationship between monster or criminal and the reader to the point where it became simultaneously unbearable and pleasurable. Perhaps this central tension of reader response explains why generations of readers continue to react to Poe's characters and their situations with mixed revulsion and secret identification. As Noël Carroll has posited in his wide-ranging exegesis of the attraction-repulsion phenomenon we associate with the horror monster: "They [monsters] are repelling . . . and also compelling of our attention. They can rivet attention and thrill for the self-same reason that they disturb, distress, and disgust" (188).

One of the most important elements that Poe inherited from his Gothic forefathers and went on to sharpen to the point of near suffocating exactitude was an emphasis on the biology of place. Walpole's castle was first in a long line of unnaturally animated buildings; from Otranto to Stephen King's Overlook Hotel in *The Shining*, the Gothic novel has always centered on hysterical characters trapped in a circumscribed space. Subterranean tunnels, intertwining passageways, and dimly lit corridors descending toward absolute darkness are standard tropes in the Gothic novel. As Frank notes, "Gothic architecture is imbued with the character and will of its former owners. Place becomes personality, as every corner and dark recess of the Gothic castle exudes a remorseless aliveness and often a vile intelligence" (14). Poe's tales of terror, and many of his detective and comic stories as well, are likewise set in Gothic architecture that is invigorated with an infernal energy of its own. But in Poe, the machinery of the haunted castle or mansion always becomes a semiotic parallel to the tortured psyche of the main character. Cut off from all external reality and menaced by his enclosing mansion, Roderick Usher's psychological deterioration, as well as the dissolution of the Usher lineage, is mirrored in the decaying physical structure of the house itself. When sister falls atop brother at the story's climax, the House of Usher itself appears to respond directly to their union, as its walls crumble and collapse upon the pair.

The male narrators in Poe's tales of terror simply cannot and do not subsist outside the physical spheres in which they dwell. In other words, Poe intensified the Gothic's configuration that linked personality and place, supplying examples of confined and subterraneous imagery with a psychodynamic correspondence to his male characters; their wills, their behavior, their very lives are both contained and symbolically represented within the terrain of their living quarters.

The paradigmatic Poe horror story displays several unifying traits, the most common of which is isolation or sequestration. "The Pit and the Pendulum," "Ligeia," "The Cask of Amontillado," "The Tell-Tale Heart," "The Masque of the Red Death," "Morella," "Berenice," "Imp of the Perverse," "Descent into the Maelstrom," "The Fall of the House of Usher," and "The Black Cat" all involve what Poe himself designated "a close circumscription of space" or a condition of isolation in which the characters are cut off from meaningful social communication. Like the eighteenth-century Gothic villain, who spends the majority of his time wandering through a labyrinth of corridors and secreted chambers in a castle or abbey, Poe's characters are decidedly antisocial beings. They develop particular missions or obsessions that become the center of their existence. Poe's male narrators heighten the psychologically-tortured consciousness that characterizes the first generation of Gothic villains. The focused fixations we discover in Poe are not merely reactions against boredom or acceptable morality, as is the case with Beckford's *Vathek* or Lewis's *The Monk* (1795), where decadent excess is a goal unto itself. Poe's antiheroes seek to escape the imprisoning reality of time and space, and only one of the protagonists, the anonymous heretic-narrator of "The Pit and the Pendulum," escapes.

In almost every case, these isolatoes are in rebellion against some restrictive moral or physical law that denies them their high poetic place in the universe. Hence, their rebellion often is concentrated upon a person or object associated with personalized restriction—a black cat, white teeth, a vulturelike eye, a blonde, blue-eyed wife. These icons of propriety must be destroyed if the narrator is to attain the sort of freedom he craves. Typically, the attempt to forge a new identity through crime is an exalting experience. After disposing of wife and cat, the narrator of "The Black Cat" announces,

"My happiness was supreme! The guilt of my dark deed disturbed me but a little . . . . I looked upon my future felicity as secured" (206). But from such pinnacles of momentary bliss, Poe's criminals descend into the lonely silence of the tomb, the jail, or the lunatic asylum.

The ubiquity of time in these clock-haunted stories—especially the convergence of the two hands of the clock at the midnight hour, the exact moment when spiritual crisis appears to intersect with physical action—represents a verticality related to the aspirations of the self, as the two-hands-become-one point the way to an identity above the material world. Poe's characters would annihilate time in order to transcend the limitations of a conventionally regulated world. Midnight is that moment in the day when time is literally suspended; it is neither yesterday, today, nor tomorrow. Most acts of criminality in Poe's microcosm occur precisely at midnight. It is at the midnight moment that Poe's murderers find their own moral prohibitions suspended. They are momentarily free to indulge their basest instincts, to act as though they were agents ungoverned by forces outside themselves—society, ethics, even time itself. For what greater restriction is there upon the desires of man than the inexorable and constantly eroding authority that time exerts?

But as the clock's hands must necessarily separate, so too must the narrator fall backward into the clock-ruled pit of time. The imposition of temporal control thwarts the creation of any self-enclosed ideality; as an objective signifier, time shatters the subjective realm fashioned by the criminal. In "The Tell-Tale Heart," for example, the narrator's initial urge to "smile gaily, to find the deed so far done," (197) is transformed into anxiety and terror when the imagined pulsations of his victim's heart are perceived as the "sound a watch makes when enveloped in cotton" (198). This collusion of sound and guilt assails the ears of the murderer, causing him to scream out to the police, a confession apparently caused less by regret than the unbearable union of time's progress with a stentorian heartbeat. What Jean-Paul Weber has labeled as Poe's "superpositions and the vertical structures" (94) cannot be sustained as the main characters come to realize that in attempting to destroy the symbols of the material world—indeed, time itself—they are in actuality destroying themselves.

The homicidal or self-destructive narrators of "The Black Cat," "The Tell-Tale Heart," "Berenice," "The Cask of Amontillado," "Imp of the Perverse," "The Purloined Letter," or "William Wilson" should be distinguished from those narrators in Poe who are haunted by women who will not die and will not stay buried. "Morella," "Ligeia," "The Fall of the House of Usher," and "Eleanora" offer us a variant to what we have seen so far in Poe's development of the psychological horror story. For unlike the often aggressive and actively contradictory nature of the male criminal, Poe's narrators who wait and watch for women to return from the dead are emasculated males who take on certain stereotypically feminine qualities in their essential passivity. The women in these tales, by contrast, are the active agents who return to haunt or punish their conscience-stricken men. Their men also appear to expect some sort of retribution, as in the case of Roderick Usher who anticipates his sister's ghastly return almost from the moment of her interment.

Joan Dayan argues that the narrators who wait for the forever beautiful, always erudite, and emotionally-charged women who have been buried prematurely or who return as lady revenants share a "specific relation of domination, where the speaker who has defined himself as possessor is in turn defined by his possession" (186). The central theme of passionate longing for immortality, especially in a woman who is less flesh and blood than etherealized being, is both a curse and an obsessional desire for the men in these tales. Yet as in his development of the horror tale, here as well Poe was unable to separate carnality from ideality, bloody acts from idealized longings. Poe's compulsive lovers, again like his criminals and murderers, always appear to embody sadomasochistic urges: they receive a particular admixture of terror and excitement from both the situation they have invariably helped to create (their curious ambivalence toward the recently deceased female who represents a constant and consuming distraction) and the particulars of their enslavement (the fact that the woman often returns, like Morella or Madeline Usher, seeking revenge). While Poe may have insisted that the "death of a beautiful woman is, unquestionably, the most poetical topic in the world" (458), the women who return from the dead in his love stories make for dangerous and angry family relatives. For reasons often not fully explained, they seek to punish husbands, brothers, and fathers for their varying levels of guilt, emotional confusion, romantic naiveté, and failure to love. No longer either loving or feminine, Poe's women return to the mortal world as antitheses of the poetical ideal Poe extolled in "The Philosophy of Composition." Always when dealing with Poe's women, passion is never very far removed from the monstrous.

Dayan posits that in those stories that begin as tales of love and end in ghastly hauntings, Poe's narrators "first look upon, idealize, and feel with the mind, hollowing out the beloved image, and then turn on the object of their affections, only to suffer retribution for their conversion" (199). This alternating pattern reflects the ambivalence that Poe's amorous narrators feel toward the feminine, but it likewise poses another similarity with the attitude his murderers come to feel toward the objects of their wrath/affection. From the old man in "The Tell-Tale Heart," who we are told, is both loved and despised, to the extremities of domestic femininity associated with the black cat in the story of the same name, the morbid obsessiveness of Poe's criminals often straddles the boundaries separating love and hate, even to the point where distinctions are altogether blurred. In both his tales of homicide and love stories, then, Poe's male narrators experience a full and contradictory spectrum of human emotions—from guilt and bereavement to elation and terror.

As the Gothic novel developed in the late eighteenth century, one of its most readily identifiable characteristics was the inclusion of a male villain. This figure, as we've already mentioned, inhabited a highly antisocial milieu and tended to express his nature in equally antisocial behavior, particularly in his antipathy toward women. But Gothic villains, from Lewis's Ambrosio to the Byronic hero, were hardly one-dimensional personalities. They were perverse admixtures of goodness aborted and greatness twisted. Stephen King himself appears to sense our close affinity with the monster when he argues in "Why We Crave Horror Movies," that "If we share a brotherhood of man, then we also share an insanity of man" (500). From his very inception the horror villain/monster was seldom wholly unsympathetic; the reader is always cognizant of the Gothic male's duality—of his tortured mind and soul, and of the potential that is thwarted in his loss of moral balance. Noël Carroll supports a multi-representational reading of the horror monster, and concludes that horror art has always undercut any theory of a unitary self: "The genre is populated by beings comprised of multiple selves or creatures undergoing disintegration" (178).

This theme of the double life or secret sharer occurs in several Poe tales, but is given its most formal expression in "William Wilson" (as well as in "The Purloined Letter," but in a different form). The narrator of the tale, the first of two characters named William Wilson, recalls the annoying presence in his life of a mysterious twin or *doppelgänger* who has haunted him since his school days. The two Wilsons are identical in physical appearance only; beyond that they are moral and intellectual opposites. One Wilson is a dissolute and perverted individual who indulges every vice and pleasure in excess. The second Wilson appears to be the superego to the first Wilson's id; he represents critical and conservative principles, and always appears to interrupt the decadent pleasures of the first Wilson. These two Wilsons do battle against one another throughout the story, until finally, at the conclusion, the evil Wilson murders his other self, plunging "my sword, with brute ferocity, repeatedly through and through his bosom." As the double dies, he pronounces judgment on the other Wilson: "'You have conquered . . . . Yet, henceforward art thou also dead—dead to the World, to Heaven and to Hope!'" (130).

These ambiguous words of condemnation suggest the full import of Poe's exploration into the psychological themes of a divided human nature. Just as we have traced evidence of Poe's concept of perversity—the contradictory sentiments that his murderers and criminals experience in the commission and punishment attendant to their crimes—the moral William Wilson warns his immoral twin that the latter cannot endure in the void of self-indulgence. In the abandonment of all constraints of conscience, the evil Wilson is liberated to pursue his predatory lifestyle with total license. But as we have seen through the evolutionary nature of crime and punishment in "The Tell-Tale Heart" and "The Black Cat," Poe continually demonstrates that human nature's true condition is divided, and that this split may underscore a certain necessary balance of opposing impulses. Eliminating the duality, the dark side becomes darker. Without a mitigating conscience, then, the unrestrained William Wilson finds himself free to join Poe's other criminal narrators in the hell of a self-designed ideality: "'see by this image, which is thine own, how utterly thou has murdered thyself'" (130). In spite of appearing to be about excess and decadence, the horror genre has, in fact, always been about transgression and movement into tabooed lands. At its most significant level of meaning, the genre offers cautionary tales concerned with detailing the fate that now awaits the liberated William Wilson: the tragic consequences of social and personal disintegration.

Within the tormented psyches of Poe's protagonists, the Gothic's emphasis on a contradictory and divided self is omnipresent. And, once again, Poe's efforts in the field only served to heighten the intensity of the genre's convention. Indeed, many writers who followed Poe—particularly those represented in this book—were drawn to his portraits of the split self. The Russian novelist Dostoevsky, for example, studied Poe's artful and artless murderers to the degree that Dostoevsky's own most memorable characters, such as Raskolnikov in *Crime and Punishment*, are Poe-esque portrayals of divided and self-disintegrating personalities. And, as we will explore in a forthcoming chapter, certainly Robert Louis Stevenson's split narrative, *The Strange Case of Dr. Jekyll and Mr. Hyde*, is an elaborate restatement of the central conflict of selfhood initially explored in "William Wilson." Both texts state a similar message: that the path to a normal, healthy life leads decidedly away from dangerous private pursuits conducted secretly in dark rooms hidden away from family and friends.

Poe's short narratives of horror and suspense offer a compressed world populated by psyches out of control. His unprecedented success at evoking conditions of intense psychological obsessiveness yielded a body of fiction that still manages to disconcert modern audiences thoroughly acclimated to audiovisual violence and gore. In high school and college curricula throughout the United States and many other cultures as well, Poe's work has maintained a high level of popularity for over a century. "Adolescence," as Leslie Fiedler reminds us, "is Poe's true homeland, the imaginary country out of space and in time of which he was, throughout his short life, a secret but loyal citizen" (199). Perhaps the adolescent reader is immediately drawn to Poe because so many of his tales and poems concern themes of lost or unrequited love, a subject that is of immediate relevance to youth experiencing such complex and ambivalent emotions for the first time. But this is an obvious connection. Bedeviled by questions of authority and identity, anxiety over social acceptance, and sexual confusion, young adults can relate as well to the violent propensities of such antiheroes as William Wilson or the narrator of "Berenice." The release of repressed energies in the form of antisocial acts underscores the tempestuous nature of adolescence in a high-achievement culture. Walter Evans reminds us in "Monster Movies: A Sexual Theory" that "the adolescent's experiences with irrational desires, fears, urges which are incomprehensible yet clearly stronger than the barriers erected by reason or society, are deeper and more painful than adults are likely to realize" (500).

Deep personal suffering is a trait that all of Poe's protagonists share in common; as outcasts, they painfully embody the adolescent's nightmare of alienation from a social fabric s/he simultaneously scorns and desperately yearns to join. The surreal nature of the writer's imagined universe coupled with the contradictory set of impulses that pit the typical Poe narrator against himself would seem to create a fictional landscape with which most teenagers might immediately identify. The urge toward self-torment and destruction and the physical elimination of others as a relief for social and sexual repression are normal conditions in Poe's abnormal world; the highly individualized torment of his characters, their anxieties and rage, pose a familiar terrain for young students beset with epidemic statistics of divorce, drug use, and teenage suicide.

The inclusion of violence and the grotesque as major themes in the tales and poems has often been read as an extension of warped sexuality and sublimated sexual response. As Marie Bonaparte was first to point out in her psychoanalytic interpretation of Poe, *The Life and Works of Edgar Allan Poe*, Poe's writing furnishes overwhelming evidence of his sexual maladjustment. His lifelong fixation on women either dead or prematurely dying in both his life and his literature suggests a man who was unable to resolve his anxieties toward women and sexuality into any kind of mature balance. This fact alone forges perhaps a final link with the terrors and tensions of adolescent puberty. Considering the appeal of Poe to the pubertal prisoner, one ambivalent reader, T. S. Eliot, observed: "The forms which his lively curiosity takes are those in which a pre-adolescent mentality delights" (212). Ironically, as Eliot recognized, Poe's most memorable work conveys us downward in a direction diametrically opposite to those zones of supernal beauty of which he was so fond and into the fatally erotic milieu of the adolescent, who must grapple with internal forces he neither understands nor is wholly capable of controlling.

As we now turn this discussion towards Poe's creation of detective fiction, perhaps the first point worth noting is that detective tales, unlike horror stories, center on the detective rather than the monster. As such, it tends to emphasize psyches under control, a necessary prerequisite to solving a crime. As a consequence, the audience for the detective tale is decidedly different from that for the tale of terror. In discussions of the audience for detection, the question most frequently asked is not, is the audience adolescent or mature, because it is usually assumed that the genre attracts a more mature readership. Rather, given this mature audience, do more men or more women read detective fiction? (cf. "Judge Lynch," "Battle of the Sexes: The Judge and His Wife Look at Mysteries," in Haycraft, *The Art of the Mystery Story* 367–72.) No one has come to any conclusions on this gender question, but what scholars of the genre seldom ask is, do adolescents read detective fiction? This is not the world of sexual tensions and adolescent rage that we have affiliated with Poe's development of the horror genre, but the rational world of the adult. It is the patterning of the world, its order, which dominates the detective story. Robert S. Paul argues that the detective story is "a fusion of the creative insights of the new romanticism with the logical analysis that had dominated the Age of Reason" (34). What the detective story searches for is "ethical enthusiasm" (Wright 66), a desire for the Neoclassical order which once existed and which could be reimposed, if only momentarily. What Poe's detective stories do is to appeal to a more sedate, older audience.

The irrational crimes and punishments of the homicidal fantasies find a counterpart in the rational crimes and punishments of the detective tales in which Poe elaborates upon the skill of the central character, C. Auguste Dupin, in employing the imagination of the poet and the analytic intelligence of the mathematician to solve insoluble crimes (see Haycraft, *Murder for Pleasure* 22–24). To crack his cases, Dupin's mind entertains a perfect balance of analysis and speculative insight rendered all the more effective by his close identification with the criminal and his thought processes. Solving the crime is not a moral act at all but an intellectual and intuitive exercise, as the writing of a beautiful poem was for Poe. Poe's detective and Poe's criminals are opposite sides of the same authorial consciousness; not coincidentally, they represent the two central opposing philosophical orientations of the eighteenth century.

Like the anonymous murderers of "The Black Cat" and "The Tell-Tale Heart," Dupin is by design self-stimulated by the exotic and the peculiar and yet acts according to a master plan. A crime, like a tale of terror, intensifies our awareness of human existence. Everyday moments lose a degree of their banality and are transformed by the sensational nature of a crime. As everything becomes a potential clue, all of life becomes charged with potential importance. Juxtaposing Dupin's deliberative methods to the criminal behavior dramatized in the horror tales we discover that the mental routine of Dupin has much in common with the inquisitive narrators of the homicidal fantasies. Completely self-contained and deigning to enter the social sphere only to exhibit his crime-solving prowess to the embarrassment of the authorities, the great detective operates on a plane above the forces of law and social convention. Because the moral implications of the crime never intrude upon the ideal solution, Dupin always succeeds where the moralists fail. Beautiful and perfect in conception and execution, his solutions are works of art as Dupin has attained the sort of ideality that both Poe's poets and theoretical killers and madmen vainly seek.

The modern detective story begins with the publication of Poe's "The Murders in the Rue Morgue" in 1841. Similar or parallel intentions can be clearly discerned in two related "tales," "The Man of the Crowd" (1840), in which the mystery refuses to be solved even through the efforts of a detective narrator, and "The Imp of the Perverse" (1845), in which the mystery will not stay quiet but bursts forth of its own volition. While both of these efforts have only vestigial plot lines (the narrator follows the man of the crowd, the narrator kills his uncle, then for no apparent reason confesses his crime), each exploits clear principles that Poe would use in his detective stories.

"The Imp of the Perverse" argues that within each person there exists not only an impulse toward the willing of his own happiness and well-being, but as well a contrary impulse, toward his own self-destruction. Poe's argument begins with the limitations of phrenology, the science of reading the bumps on one's head as a guide to the personality within. No more rational explanation for man's behavior can be found. If the part of one's brain that controls eating was more developed, it would cause a swelling in the skull. This bump of aliminitiveness would drive its possessor to eat: the larger the bump, the more one eats. Other swellings would guide the phrenologist to other tendencies: the need for friends, for reproduction, for combat. A chart of the bumps on one's head would be a map of one's behavior. Phrenology's logic appealed to the scientific side of the nineteenth century since it posited clearly identifiable causes and effects. Man did things because his brain controlled him; the shape of his brain indicated what the individual would do. The entire system seemed to be devised by a rational Divine Creator. Such a scheme would be compatible with the eighteenth-century's Age of Reason.

But Poe sensed that something was wrong; like his admirer Dosteovsky in *Notes from Underground,* he posited a contrary impulse towards evil and unhappiness which he felt the phrenologists had missed. There was no necessity for such an impulse. Poe observed that man often acted against his best interests; he suggests that the phrenologists would have been better off observing how man did act rather than declaring how man should act (226). In other words, Poe insists that any epistomological discussion must make room for the irrational, for the defiance of God in a system which was originally set up to illustrate God's lucidity. Poe dramatized this irrationality in the horror story, "The Black Cat," as well as in the prototypical detective story, "The Imp of the Perverse." The difference between the stories is that in "The Black Cat" irrationality breaks through, overwhelming the characters with the cat's cry, which is in part the verbalization of the narrator's self-torment and urge to be caught and punished for his crime, while in "The Imp of the Perverse" the desire for conventional justice takes control over the irrational.

In "The Imp of the Perverse" Poe, in an effort to understand the impulse toward self-destructiveness, personifies it. After describing examples of this urge toward self-destruction, the narrator gives it a name: The Imp of the Perverse, as well as a hand and a voice. After having ingeniously poisoned his uncle with a tainted candle burning inside a locked room, the narrator enjoys the fruits of his inheritance "for years" (229): he feels no remorse. But then he comes under the power of the Imp; he feels an urge to confess. As we have traced in several of Poe's horror tales, the ego of the criminal is often counterbalanced by the desire for punishment. Knowing he is helpless before this impulse, the narrator flees until overtaken and restrained. The narrator chokes upon the secret, which literally suffocates him; he does not want to say the words which will condemn him to the hangman. But some invisible fiend strikes him with "his broad palm upon the back," and the secret bursts forth as if it had a life of its own. While we neither see nor hear the Imp, we feel its hand on the narrator. We recognize the same impulse within ourselves: as in the horror story, some force within ourselves over which we have no control wants us to reveal our darkest secrets, to repudiate our worst crimes.

In "The Imp of the Perverse," we gain initial insight into the importance of murder to the detective tale; it is, as W. H. Auden points out in "The Guilty Vicarage," the one deed which society must avenge because it abolishes the party it injures. We also find the most frequent motive—money—and an ingenious locked room mystery. While suspense is ignored and there is no detective hero, it is a gem of a tale illustrating the larger themes of man's urge to self-destruction and the attempt at control through knowledge about the impulse to do evil.

On the other hand, "The Man of the Crowd" does not offer a specific crime to be solved nor does it come to rest in any moral certainty but in moral ambiguity: evil lives in the heart of the crowd. It is the tale of the "devil-in-our-midst." It shows a detective, an amateur, a hypersensitive young man, like other Poe characters such as Roderick Usher and C. Auguste Dupin, who is primarily an observer of what goes on around him. He sees, knows, and imagines more than he should be able to. He observes the classes into which all mankind falls, seeing the stereotypes of clerks old and young, of pickpockets, card sharps, Jew pedlars, street beggars, through those who haunt the edges of the night. Only by examining these stereotypes can he discover the great individual, the man of the crowd, whose mystery is beyond comprehension. The detective "leaps up in pursuit, but the man is elusive in every sense: he never stops, never breaks away from the city's milling crowds. All he does is walk, day and night. The café detective eventually gives up his chase" (Ross 76–79, 78) and the essence of all crime is undivulged. This type of the criminal, sprung from Cain, the father of all crime, stands for the Other, the adversary, he who denies and defies. He finds his truest literary parallel in the figure of the monster, who haunts the Gothic tale of terror. In the detective story, this individual will be the one to be overcome, Professor Moriarty, or the Minister D_____.

"The Man of the Crowd" represents the mystery which each of us wishes to understand, the puzzle which we pursue to its conclusion. In the horror story, we overcome the threat of the unknown by locating it in ourselves or in our society; in the detective story, we overcome the threat by placing it in an objective moral context and punishing the perpetrator who is, after all, not ourselves. In this story, however, "the mystery does not allow itself to be read" (139).

But the great detective, C. Auguste Dupin, solves all mysteries. In the three Poe stories in which he appears, Dupin solves two murders and saves his country's queen from political blackmail. In the first story, "The Murders in the Rue Morgue," (1841) we meet Dupin through the eyes of an unnamed narrator, well-educated, a good writer, a keen observer, but slow to pick up on clues. Thus Dupin can explain to him—and through him to the reader—how he arrives at his conclusions. The narrator is astounded and conveys his astonishment at Dupin's powers of ratiocination to the reader.

Dupin, in "The Murders in the Rue Morgue," illustrates the power of analysis and speculative insight to overcome the irrational, the mind controlling what it understands. Dupin is part logician, part Romantic poet, and part metaphysician, but his supreme crime-solving gift is his imagination, which enables him to identify with the criminal mind. Like the anonymous murderers of "The Black Cat" and "The Tell-Tale Heart," Dupin is by Poe's design self-stimulated by the exotic and peculiar, and acts according to a master plan. The mental routine of Dupin has much in common with the inquisitive narrators we have traced from the homicidal fantasies. But where the narrators from Poe's horror stories always verged toward and eventually embodied irrational principles, Dupin is in possession of the sharpest mental faculties, or ratiocination, that permits him to stay in absolute control of himself and the situation.

As the various and contradictory witnesses are brought forth to provide testimony in "The Murders in the Rue Morgue," Dupin concludes that the voice heard by each of the witnesses was not human. The apparently confusing testimony of the witnesses is brought under control by Dupin's mind to yield its kernel of truth. What looked chaotic is converted into useful information for the detective.

Dupin examines the scene of the double murder. He explains to the narrator that all the outré details, those which confuse the ordinary observer, make the crime easier to solve through the powers of analysis. He follows the links of his chain of reasoning till they lead him to the nail, the clue to the means of egress from the locked murder chamber. He repeats that he has not once been "at fault"; therefore, he cannot be wrong. Through analysis he solves a pair of murders committed by an irrational beast. If this were a horror tale, the orang-outang might have escaped, remaining at large to haunt the dreams of law-abiding citizens. Instead, the beast is captured and put safely into a zoo.

The horrific details of the murder—one body stuffed up the chimney with such force that it takes two men to free it, a second with its throat so severely slashed that the head falls off when the body is raised—are worthy of the horror tale. So is the murder chamber, on the fourth floor (fifth floor in American practice) in the rear, where one should feel safe from the intrusion of predators. The victims too are women (as they are in all Poe's detective tales and many of his horror stories) whose helplessness is not respected, and whose victimization, as in the horror tales, makes their fate so much more shocking.

Poe's sense of setting, of the "close circumscription of space" (460) he posits in "The Philosophy of Composition" and applies dramatically to help intensify the terror of his psychological horror tales, is created by the locked room mystery (which Poe also used in "The Imp of the Perverse"). The question is, how did the murderer gain access to, and escape from, the murder chamber when the only way out is blocked by the crowd attracted by the screams of the death agonies of the two women? As in the horror tale, the closed space allows the labyrinth of the mind to engulf the reader. We follow the trail through seemingly trackless paths until logic and the clarity of reason triumph over the forces of violence and terror. The closeness of space suffocates us until we burst through to the solution, feeling lucky to have escaped the horror through the help of the detective.

In "The Mystery of Marie Roget," a weaker story, the distinction between narrator and actor is obscured; comments from "Mr. Poe" suggest that he is the narrator. But the long lecture by Dupin on his inferences from the clues and his explanation of the "Calculus of Probabilities" leads to his conclusion that the murder was not done by a gang, that it was a personal crime, and that the advice of the detective, rightfully followed, would reveal the murderer. This story is held back by its insistence on blunting the dramatic possibilities and allowing the narrative force to be carried by the reasoning of Dupin, who turns out to be an exhaustive and exhausting lecturer. Unlike "The Murders in the Rue Morgue" or "The Purloined Letter," there is no struggle with the incompetent police; they are kept in the background. There is little inter-reaction between Dupin and the narrator. The only dramatic tension in "The Mystery of Marie Roget" comes from Dupin criticizing the newspapers to show how wrong their speculations must be. Except for the phrase "calculus of probabilities," borrowed later by Holmes in *The Hound of the Baskervilles* to pursue the author of the note warning Henry Baskerville away from his ancestral home, Poe's story contributes little to the development of the form.

In "The Purloined Letter," Poe clearly identifies his detective with the criminal, showing that one mind struggles successfully with another only through identifying with it. According to Leroy Lad Panek, one of Poe's major contributions to the creation of the detective story was the creation of a worthy antagonist for Dupin; their competition gives this story its verve and life (30). Part of this competition arises from Poe's insistence on games and games theory. In "The Murders in the Rue Morgue," Poe discusses the games of chess and draughts and describes how to win at the game of whist: the player "throws himself into the spirit of his opponent, identifies himself therewith," and figures out how to overcome his rival. Dupin gives the same advice in "The Purloined Letter" in describing the game of "even and odd." The young man who wins all the marbles in his school wins by identifying his "intellect with that of his opponent" (217). Dupin also defeats the Minister by using this technique.

Indeed, the intellects of both men, Dupin and Minister D_____, are identified in many ways. When the Prefect of Police says that the Minister is "only one remove from a fool," being a poet, Dupin confesses, "I have been guilty of certain doggerel myself" (212). Dupin, like Poe himself, understands that while poetry is not typically an aid to criminal investigations, the poet's powers of intuition and imagination make him a worthy adversary for any criminal mind. In fact, it is because the poet possesses such attributes that he is capable of intellectual insights unavailable to the imaginatively retarded Prefect.

Dupin and the Minister have been acquainted before since the Minister did Dupin an evil turn once in Vienna. Dupin's solution of where the letter was hidden, and his leaving a clue to his identity in the false letter, is part of the game they play, a game with the serious consequences of political ruin for Minister D_____. Dupin's clue, which he leaves in the false letter, says in effect that the plot is worthy of Atreus or of Thyestes, of Dupin or his opponent Minister D_____, completes the identification of the two players. Indeed, it should come as no surprise if we were to discover that the Minister's full name is "Dupin," the mirror image which we have traced in "William Wilson" (cf. Hayford, *Murder* 22–24).

This splitting of the detective and the criminal into two parts of the same character comes from the same impulse that Poe used to split William Wilson into two parts. While this divided personality, this secret sharer, unlike William Wilson, does not look the same, they do, however, think the same. While they have known each other, and perhaps share the same name as well as the same impulse toward writing poetry, they differ in their intentions. The Minister is a politician, therefore seeking to advance his own range of power. He purloins the letter in order to gain precedence over the Queen, to force her to use her voice to promote his political ends. Dupin is not only on the side of law and order, assisting the Prefect of Police, but backs up the Queen and the existing political status quo. By hiding the fact that the letter is no longer at his disposal, Dupin causes the Minister to fall from the heights of success. The latter's fall is as ignominious as that awaiting William Wilson, in the world without his double.

Through this identification, Dupin deduces that the Minister would choose to hide the letter in plain sight. Significantly, Dupin uses another game, the map game, to explain how he can discover the letter which the Prefect, with all his pains, cannot. The police work on a different level from either Dupin or the Minister and completely miss the letter. Dupin, however, does not use logic, as he did in "The Murders in the Rue Morgue," to find the letter. Instead, he relies upon the observational skills of a poet to note that the letter is radically different from the methodical habits of D_____; it was carelessly displayed, dirty, and crumpled. But all the other details of the letter were the opposite of what had been described to Dupin: the address, the handwriting, and seal. In identifying his intellect with that of the Minister, he swiftly comes to the conclusion that this is the letter. One does not display logic by saying, this is what I seek because it is so different from what I seek. It is the identification of the intellects who choose the same method that solves the mystery.

In the horror story the monster comes either from within society or from within the main protagonist in some symbolic fashion. The drive in the horror story is to understand where the monster has come from and how to control it. Eventually, the horror tale often comes to acknowledge that hero and monster share unequivocal similarities, e.g., Frankenstein and his creature, Jekyll and his Hyde. But usually this insight is reserved exclusively for the reader to conclude; the hero fights such affiliations to his very death. The monster is always "other" from the main protagonist's point of view. The creature comes from some other world than the one the hero inhabits. In the detective tale, this gap seldom exists. The murderer and the detective inhabit the same world, whether the upper class world of Agatha Christie or the mean streets of Raymond Chandler. Both Dupin and Minister D_____ come from the same social class, the same educational background, and have been trained to think in a particular way. It is their similarities that impress the reader.

What the detective story looks for, as amply illustrated by "The Purloined Letter," is balance. Dupin and the Minister are balanced in the way in which their minds work: the Minister threatens the Queen with the possession of her letter and is brought down by his lack of knowing that the letter has been taken and another substituted; both the Queen and the Minister hide the letter in plain sight. Even the qualities of the letter, opposite to those the Prefect has described, are balanced off with their opposing characteristics of address and seal.

Romanticism, as we have earlier noted, contains within itself an impulse toward the untidy and the imprecise; it is this same impulse that gives birth to both horror and detection: how can one deal with the essential mystery at the heart of things? The horror tale pursues the extreme in an exhausting search into the self, exploring the darkness that also makes us human. The detective tale acknowledges the existence of human evil, but then pulls back, seeking control in order to restrain the extreme. Modeling itself after the Enlightenment more than the Gothic impulse toward annihilation, the detective story searches for moral containment and rational judgment. A controlled and balanced world may prove ephemeral, but its pursuit gives a sense of closure and satisfaction that is often lacking in the horror tale. In the horror tale, we are left with a monster unleashed from within ourselves or upon our society; in the detective tale we are left with the criminal punished in some appropriate fashion that leaves the reader with a greater sense of security. We search for some balance between the impulse to destroy and the impulse to preserve. Both impulses are part of what it means to be human, and both represent the two major artistic legacies Poe's children inherited from their literary father.

Chapter 2
Poe's Children:
The Conjunction of the Detective and Gothic Tales

"Next time you'll tell me two things. What happened with the
horse is one. The other thing I wonder is . . . how do you manage
your rage?" (Harris, *The Silence of the Lambs* 155)

This question put by Doctor Hannibal "The Cannibal" Lecter to Clarice
Starling is one that could be asked of anyone in today's society: how do
we manage to deal with a world increasingly filled with violence, with
killings explained away by such statements as he's a "nice guy": "There's
nothing wrong with John [Salvi, who killed two clerks and wounded
others in clinics which provide abortions] whatsoever other than he killed
a couple people" (Trott 1). How do we explain what happened to this "nice
guy," how do we uncover who he really is, how do we gain enough
insight into his "secret self" to help us understand why he resorted to violent behavior? And perhaps most disturbing of all, what circumstances
would be necessary to make any one of us respond in a similar manner?

Edgar Allan Poe faced these same issues in his own lifetime: how to
respond to the growing violence of an increasingly violent nineteenth-
century America. He used two methods, both of which have had important consequences for popular fiction. One way was to transfer such pervasive horrors into Gothic tales, such as "The Tell-Tale Heart," which
delineates a violent homicide that ends up destroying both the perpetrator
and his victim. This narrative manages to explore three uniquely different
vantage points for apprehending terror: that felt by the murderer as he
anticipates and then carries out the homicide, that projected upon the victim (in the murderer's mind) at the moment he is surprised, and that felt
by the reader in serving as witness to this senseless killing. In short narratives, from "William Wilson" to "The Fall of the House of Usher," Poe
details the contradictions of the human mind, the interior battle between
self-control and perversity that provides at least partial insight into the two-
sidedness of John Salvi. In Poe, surrendering rational controls, either
through self-indulgence or through depreciation of another's life, leads to
a chaotic, incomprehensible, but nonetheless passionately-felt existence;
his characters feel most alive when they are engaged in various acts of
destruction and depravity.

But another side of Poe was also interested in formulating a method-
ology for containing or constructively sublimating the violent energies of
the self. Through the invention of the detective tale, C. Auguste Dupin
deals with the irrational violence represented by the ourang-outang in "The

Murders in the Rue Morgue" and with the dangers of human predators in "The Purloined Letter." In other words, Poe explores the concept of violence narratologically by objectifying it, by putting it in someone else's head, as in the horror tale; or, he exercises control of it through his alter ego, Dupin. The Gothic describes a dissolving world in which the horror comes close to triumph; the detective tale takes charge of a world whose rationality contains and controls the horror.

In his famous discussion of Dionysian energies and Apollonian counterbalances, Friedrich Nietzsche wrote that "The Greeks were keenly aware of the terrors and horrors of existence; in order to be able to live at all they had to place before them the shining fantasy of the Olympians" (553). Nietzsche suggests two ways of dealing with the horrors of existence which find appropriate narrative parallels in Poe. The first of these is Apollonian, the fantasy of the Olympians. This was the dream of rational order, akin to that imposed by the detective on the world around him. It represents a realm of perimeters, of happiness suggested by a world at least temporarily at peace. This fantasy is underlined by the assurance that each reader of detective fiction possesses: that he or she is consciously reading a fiction as a fiction, one which will end, if not happily, at least with the problem resolved, a situation acknowledged by both reader and author.

The horror tale, on the other hand, takes its cue from the seductive elements of the Dionysian myth, where the reader is encouraged to forsake the safe havens of the detective narrative and venture beyond into a landscape that is often both illicit and protean. The horror story contains energies that are so evocative precisely because they are dangerous and disruptive, exploring a world without limits, a world of extravagance. That is one of the reasons Poe's horror tales seldom end with a clear resolution; we are left to wonder exactly how Ligeia (or the narrator) managed to reanimate Lady Rowena's corpse, or what Berenice might have said to the narrator as she came in the door, her teeth scattered on the narrator's desk.

The abolition of limits is one of the most powerful impulses found in Poe. He understood this as an artist, writing more horror stories than detective tales, as well as a man, by allowing alcoholism to confound both his professional and private lives. The intoxication of the narrator of "The Pit and the Pendulum," as he reels and almost falls into the pit which he has been so sedulous to avoid, betrays a sense of confusion, horror, and escape, all at once. Even when Poe chooses to end a story in the condemned man's cell, as in "The Black Cat," the narrator is left in a place without clearly defined perimeters: "Today I am here. But tomorrow where?" Nietzsche suggests that it is in the uniting of the Apollonian and the Dionysian that the creation of art occurs, in the struggle between two oppositional impulses. In these terms at least, Poe's vision of art is similarly unified since it provides two ways of dealing with "the terrors and horrors of existence": the detective story moves toward order and resolution, the horror tale toward intoxication and abandonment. If Poe uses both these genres to explore a personal and an artistic awareness of rage, how do they interconnect? If these forms differ, they still have a great deal in common because they try to confront the same evil at the heart of the human condition.

One way we can analyze these two forms is to turn to W. H. Auden's classic analysis of the English detective story, "The Guilty Vicarage." Auden writes that the detective story brings the reader, in a moral fashion, from false to true innocence, with the discovery and the elimination of murder (sin or horror). Both detective and horror fiction, with slight variations, begin in a state of relative calm that is abruptly broken when the murder is committed or the evil force released. There may be more variations in the detective story: the murder may have been committed before the story begins, the story may open with the murder, or the murder takes place after the story is well under way. The gothic usually begins in a peaceful state, as in Stephen King's middle-class families and friendships, but there are clear strains which exist even within these seemingly placid domestic relationships. But these are revealed in the next stage of exposition.

The murder or the unleashing of horror is largely a revelatory process: its respective seeds await new growth in the falsely innocent state that begins each genre. In the detective story, the motive for murder exists within the falsely peaceful state; the criminal/monster may be loose but not yet noticed. In the horror story, the evil that is released is something out of control, something chaotic, but the main characters have to feel the full impact of its presence. In the detective story, the detective may seem either to have lost the thread of his deductions or be at the mercy of forces that may prove to be stronger than he is. However, in the detective story, the detective is always the central figure, the one whom we follow and whose ultimate control we never doubt. Even when Sherlock Holmes momentarily despairs at a new turn in the case, as he does in *The Hound of the Baskervilles* when he mistakes the identity of the corpse of the convict Selden for that of his client (419–20), we are confident that all will be well in the end. At the conclusion of that novel, when Sir Henry Baskerville is almost overcome in the fog, one of the reasons for his unstable condition is the supposed supernatural origin of the hound that pursues him. But since this is a detective and not a horror tale, we never doubt that reason will win out in the end and the supernatural dissipated when the hound is killed by real bullets.

The main figure in the horror story is much more at the mercy of the forces of horror, of the irrational. He or she inhabits an environment that is out of control. Particularly in the modern horror story, the growing sense of unreality takes the reader step by step into a world where nothing is secure. In traditional pre-1960 horror fiction, the monster never really looks like a human being. There is always something to set him apart: dress, body distortion, animal appearance. Since then, however, the monster has transformed into a seemingly "more human" representative—the psychopath who is seething on the inside, but one of us on the outside. As film scholar Robin Wood has detailed, the horror monster has always horrified us with his evil at the same time as he delights us with his audacity; while part of us is appalled by his excesses and outrages, another part gleefully identifies with his rebellion against social, sexual, and moral codes of acceptable behavior (80). As we anticipate the destruction of the monster with great anxiety, we also sense—if not recognize—that he is acting out our own darkest impulses to violate taboos and act without fear of retribution.

Few works of horror have totally unsympathetic monsters. When Mary Shelley wrote *Frankenstein* in 1818, her intention was to produce a tragic figure who became monstrous as a desperate reaction to his socially-constructed monstrosity. The creature, who desires only to attain some level of acceptance in the world—"'a wife for his bosom, and each beast have his mate'" (160)—to combat his human estrangement, is always more victim than victimizer. His attacks upon Frankenstein, his family, and fiancée are stimulated by frustration and despair rather than an innate depravity. Shelley's monster is the prototype for the genre, as his existential lament reverberates through the Byronic hero, is echoed in the falls of Hawthorne's misguided idealists, and resounds throughout the twentieth century. Thus, the most compelling character in Thomas Harris's novels remains the tortured tormentor, Hannibal Lecter, while Jack Nicholson's portrait of Jack Torrance remains the most memorable figure in all the films that have been made of Stephen King's fiction. Even Hollywood's monsters from the slasher genre—Leatherface, Candyman, Jason, Michael Myers (Freddy Krueger remains a notable exception)—elicit a certain level of sympathy from the audience; these are human beings who have become creatures because they have been stripped of their humanity by oppressive families, harsh and exclusionary social codes, and an omnipresent atmosphere of sexual violence.

Reconfiguring the boundaries that distinguish good from evil, horror monsters actually work to help define who we are by offering us an inverted portrait of ourselves. The Other illuminates what we keep in the shadows—both as a culture and as individuals. We find in *The Shining's* Jack Torrance a human monster whose life's meaning is reduced to the act of murdering his family, and we applaud when he fails one last time to satisfy yet another of his ill-starred quests. But there is also much about Torrance that whispers seductively to us, particularly when he is at his darkest and most pathetic: his relentless desire for fame, his alcoholic and sexual distractions, his struggle to find a viable place in the world, his inability to counterbalance lingering childhood traumas with a love for wife and child. In essence, Torrance the monster is never very far removed from Torrance the loving husband and father. Audiences may find satisfaction in his demise, but if we are fair in our assessment, we also recognize that the same destructive compulsions that transformed Jack into a monster are also present within ourselves. And, in the end, we are spared his fate perhaps more by good fortune than by imposed design.

The criminal in the detective story has often been identified with the detective, either taking his name, as the criminal does to the cab driver in *The Hound of the Baskervilles*, or in some way being the equal of the detective. In "The Purloined Letter," Poe makes it clear that C. Auguste Dupin and the Minister D_____ are equal adversaries by the note he leaves in the substitute letter at the end of the story. Sherlock Holmes is matched in evil by the nefarious Dr. Moriarty, and this equality is spelled out in the fact that both go over the Reichenbach Falls, both appear to die, yet both live. In more modern stories, where there is less of a game going on between detective and criminal, they are often not so easily identified. But these connections remain, as in the identifications of Mark Messinger and Robert Dietz, or in the competition between Jack Crawford and Hannibal Lecter to exert the greater influence upon Clarice Starling.

Some have suggested, in psychological fashion, that we read detective stories to act out in our own minds, with part of our being, the desire to murder someone, and, with another part, the desire to punish the murderer. Thus, our divided selves revel in both parts of the chase, both trying to escape capture and trying to effect capture. The detective story, in satisfying both these desires, brings to us a cathartic calm and peace which we did not have before we read the piece.

Horror art mimics similar subliminal urges, reflective of personal and cultural anxieties that are at once repressed and simultaneously indulged vicariously through the action of the horror narrative. Typically, as many psychoanalytic critics have already noticed, horror art has always been concerned with describing what is most repressed in Western culture: sexuality. Since the monster is the essential representation of that which horrifies us, it follows that the presence of horror is often in some way involved with indulging behavior associated with the id: the genre's inimitable ability to reflect the reader/audience's sexual excitements as well as sexual dreads. The pleasure principle gone askew, that which has been repressed is transformed into some kind of distorted personification. Thus, the civilized human gives way to the wolf, the sophisticate gives way to the vampire, Jekyll gives way to Hyde, the urbane psychiatrist gives way to Hannibal the Cannibal. In each case, it is the repressed figure transformed into the Other, the personification of our closeted side, which stirs our deepest fears. Yet, we greet this Other with a mixture of secret identification and repudiation, a mixture reminiscent of the divided self we feel in the detective genre when we identify simultaneously with murderer and detective. The Gothic has always inspired fear and desire at the same time: fear of and a desire for Otherness, fear of and a desire for that which we find most repulsive, fear of and a desire for the latent perversity that lurks within us all.

As we explored in the preceding chapter's discussion of Poe's connection to adolescence, the audience for horror art in general is likewise composed of a large teenage representation: in the midst of experiencing great hormonal changes that are further complicated by questions of authority and identity, teenagers appear to understand quite well the admixture of terror and liberation associated with the horror monster's physical transformation and social rebellion. The audience for the detective story is generally more advanced in years. The detective story does not give way so completely to the unbridled passions and anxieties of the young. Instead, the world, even that of the mean streets, is generally more comprehensible and more objectively recognizable than that of the horror story. Writers—and readers—retain more control over what is going on.

No matter how horrible the crime, the detective is there to take charge of the situation. Dupin grasps one end of the chain of reason and follows it link by link to its inevitable end, never once breaking the logic. Even the irrational behavior of an ourang-outang, entering and exiting a fourth-story window to commit a random and heinous double homicide in Poe's "The Murders in the Rue Morgue," is not enough to defeat our detective. The ape will be traced back to its owner, it will be captured, and it will be safely imprisoned in a zoo, never again to escape. The monster of horror, on the other hand, can always return, and as contemporary remakes of classic horror films from the 1930s and 1940s as well as the deathless slasher sequels *Friday the 13th, Halloween,* and *Nightmare on Elm Street* illustrate, he often does. Because the horror monster is so often an archetype, it never dies. On the other hand, the culprit in the detective story rarely reappears. Professor Moriarty, in the Holmes stories, appears to be a notable exception to this rule, and in this context it is interesting to note that he takes on many of the characteristics of the horror monster as well as those of the typical criminal in a detective narrative.

The monster in the horror tale is not merely a product of repression, but also a protest against it. In this way the horror genre recognizes what's wrong with society, but expresses solutions in destructive rather than constructive terms, through threatening to wreck the whole structure rather than working to modify it or make it better. Thus, on one level, the horror genre is a force for liberation that attacks the social status quo and bourgeois morality. Its art can be seen as an ideological first step toward challenging the failures of exclusionary social codes and institutions.

On the other hand, horror is also a highly conservative genre that, like the detective tale and other forms of popular literature, accepts the codes of society and strives to maintain the status quo through ostracizing and punishing the deviant monster, the distorted Other. In the typical horror story, disruptions to the norm thwart the rational inclinations of society and self. When these chaotic forces are in control, the supernatural inflicts its fury on the human world in the form of either mass disorder or a highly personal attack upon the protagonist's psyche. In the working out of this disruptive tension, however, the horror story reinstates the conventions of the acceptable. Although perhaps diminished as a consequence of what it has lost in this struggle, the horror tale nonetheless reasserts certain moral priorities and social norms.

The conservative nature of the detective tale parallels the essential narrative dynamic found in the horror tale. Following Auden's paradigm, the detective tale begins in a state of false innocence and moves toward true innocence through the exposure of the murderer and, along with the murderer, other, more minor, sins against society. Papa Poirot, as Hercule Poirot styles himself in *The Murder of Roger Ackroyd*, is a putative priest, absolving each of the characters in turn of those sins while eliminating them as suspects. Murder is the only sin that we can all agree to condemn unreservedly. Even when a murder seems justified because of the earlier acts of the victims, as in Arthur Conan Doyle's *A Study in Scarlet*, the reader is convinced that murder is wrong, and the murderer deserving of punishment. The person who commits the crime, no matter how ordinary, becomes the monstrous Other by crossing over this moral line. Murders may be clean and quiet, or ghastly and sexual, or even as perverted as the acts of the horror story, but they are all wrong. The thrill in the detective story is not to be found in the various ways in which murder may be carried out, which is often the main focus of attention in some forms of horror (e.g., splatterpunk and the slasher film), but in the thrill of the chase and its successful conclusion in the apprehension of the murderer. Whether the society depicted is the small English country town or the mean streets of an American big city, the emphasis in the detective tale is on the restoration of a comprehensible morality. This restoration results not in the reformation of society, but in the re-establishment of what existed before, in the *status quo ante*.

The murderer in the detective story is clearly recognizable; not distorted by the censoring conscious mind, the criminal is always one of us. That is one of the reasons that S. S. Van Dine's rules for the detective story say that servants are not allowed to have committed the murder (191). Servants are not one of us, or at least a member of our social class; he or she is, instead, despite any secrets in the past, limited to what we want them to do. My servant can only do those things which I am allowed to order him to do. Even Hyde is not a servant of Jekyll—an alternative available to Stevenson which he wisely did not choose to take—but a member of the same class. His monstrousness horrifies the more conventional Utterson and Enfield precisely because a member of their own class proves capable of carrying out such offensive acts. While the detective story is traditionally as patriarchal as the horror story, it is not as sexual in what it expresses or disguises. One of the reasons Poe's horror stories are so powerful is that they carry the power of disguised sexuality. The unholy union between Roderick and Madeline Usher represents, among other sins, that of incest, and their death seems accompanied by a kind of orgasmic spasm. The narrator in "The Tell-Tale Heart" is obsessed with the eye of his victim with much the same intensity as that of a fetishist who pursues his fetish. The detective story exerts control both over the forbidden desires of the id as well as over the more rational desires of the ego-murderer. Christie insists that the world of the detective is rational by claiming that there are only four motives for murder: fear, greed, hatred, and envy (Panek, *Shepards* 48). Murder cannot be committed for irrational ends, for then it would be beyond the power of the detective to find the murderer through logical means. The detective's prayer—please don't let the murderer be a crazy—is exactly the opposite of what we look for in the horror story: the crazier, the better. It is in its excess that the horror story makes its point; it is only in the act of denying human excess that the detective story exists at all.

Both horror and detective stories are formulaic; that is, they adhere closely to certain paradigmatic structures. While all literature is generally formulaic, employing forms that its audience recognizes and produces more or less a variation on what is already familiar, horror and detection follow and repeat their own conventions even more closely than other literary genres. In fact, George Dove notes that Poe impressed a genetic code for detection upon his first effort in the genre, "The Murders in the Rue Morgue": there is a detective-protagonist, there is a detection plot which is basic to the narrative, there is a problem to be solved, and there is a solution which is always reached before the story ends (23). These elements exist in all detective tales, each of which, in its narrative progression, fulfills the reader's expectations in familiar ways. One illustration of these conventions at work is the concept of the "Death Warrant," in which someone calls the detective with information crucial to the solution to the case which will be given to the detective at a later meeting. The person who will supply that information will surely be dead before the information is communicated. While Dove suggests seven steps to the process (84), there are variations that make each tale interesting to the reader. In David Housewright's *Penance*, a receptionist calls the investigator with certain knowledge of who the murderer is. When he reaches her home, he discovers her body murdered in a particularly brutal manner. In the film *Chinatown*, the woman posing as Mrs. Mulwray, Ida Sessions, first calls to say she had nothing to do with the murder. Later, the detective Jake Gittes, receives a phone call in the middle of the night saying Ida Sessions wants to talk to him. When Gittes arrives at her home, he discovers that she is dead and that the police, having found his phone number written near the phone, had called Gittes to find out how he was involved, thus shifting the homicidal investigation towards Gittes himself while also withholding any information Sessions, already dead, might have had for him.

Some suggest that such formulas show the limitations of detective and other popular fiction. But their popularity and their pervasiveness suggest that the formula is part of the enduring fascination these forms possess. Readers can go to the detective story, following Poe's lead, knowing that a solution will be found before the story's end. While there are variations, as when the Continental Op solves the murder, but can pin it on the murderer only by framing him in "The Golden Horseshoe," or when we are not sure of who the murderer is, but we know that she has been punished in Martha Grimes's *The Five Bells and Bladebone*, the reader is certain that all curiosity will be satisfied and a firm sense of closure will be delivered. Readers of detective fiction find pleasure in the variations, solidity in their inevitability, and interest in the ways the stories reflect their own times and their own concerns.

In "The Philosophy of Composition," Poe suggests that an enclosed locale or narrow space is a precondition for the proper evocation of terror. Since the other writers considered in this book are all children of Poe, they would necessarily subscribe to a similar theory of terror. The horror tale began within the tightly enclosed physical realm of *The Castle of Otranto*'s subterranean passageways, and became an even more compressed arena in Poe's narratives and the work of his Gothic progeny.

"A close circumscription of space," however, is not always a prerequisite for all terror tales; Hawthorne's deeply-wooded New England forests or the arctic expanse that is the setting for the conclusion of *Frankenstein* are cases in point. While a sense of place is always important in defining the Gothic tale, the range of places where horror occurs often indicates the *type* of terror evoked. As we discussed in the preceding chapter, Poe's narrow enclosures and premature burials are metaphors for the mind under siege; "The Tell-Tale Heart" or "The Pit and the Pendulum" center on issues of suffocation—physiological asphyxiation, of course, but also a corresponding sense of psychic and moral self-depletion as well. In horror art less obsessed with Poe-like enclosures, the modern slasher film is a good example; terror is evoked not from within—that is, in the ever-narrowing condition of the mind's threat of self-extinction—but from without.

Poe's highly internalized "cerebral Gothic" finds its generic opposite in the slasher film's fascination with the external body. In place of the inexorable enclosures that demarcate and heighten terror in Poe, the slasher film emphasizes the open wound of the broken body, the resplendently appointed corpse that *opens out*, like one of Francis Bacon's paintings, to display itself as a visual feast. Since the body is the object of assault more than the mind, films such as *Friday the 13th, The Texas Chainsaw Massacre*, and their many incestual sequels are correspondingly set in open spaces: a campground/homestead located in deep forests far from civilization, the empty expanses of concrete interstate highways that measure the vast lengths between American towns. Within this world of raw nature untouched by urban cynicism, teenage protagonists are systematically dispatched by serial killers, Jason in *Friday* and Leatherface in *Texas*. Their victims are indistinguishable from one another; by the end of these films there are so many corpses that the teenagers are reduced to gendered slabs of beef. As Jonathan Lake Crane notes, "Only when inscribed with Jason's signature do bodies acquire any meaningful or notable mark of difference. Only in death, reduced to shattered viscera, do victims become truly worthy of our undivided attention" (148).

As a consequence, the audience's response to the terror of the slasher film is markedly different from the strong personal intimacy we come to experience with murder and murdering in Poe. The victims of the slasher film are anonymous dead; they are any white, middle-class, heterosexual adolescent. Indeed, even the multiple plots of the *Friday* saga tend to blur into one another and ultimately are rendered identityless and inconsequential. Correspondingly, Jason and Leatherface, the monsters, are just as anonymous as their victims. Hidden behind omnipresent masks and brandishing large lethal weapons of penetration, we know as little about Jason's and Leatherface's sociopathic motivations as we do about the children they feel compelled to assault. Again, the emphases of these films are on an outer, rather than inner, perspective and reality. Thus, the audience for the contemporary slasher movie responds to the terror of special effects: how many dead and how original/gruesome their dismemberment.

In Poe's narratives, the reader seldom, if ever, identifies with the victim; Lady Rowena and Fortunato are surely unfortunate, as they are in the wrong place at the wrong time, but Poe's deliberately limited narratological point of view necessarily restricts our sympathies. In the case of the protagonist in "The Pit and the Pendulum," while the story is told from his perspective, readers become so enraptured by his seductively descriptive torments that they remain more interested in their exquisite detailing than in the survival of the narrator. In contrast, the modern slasher film, as Carol Clover has carefully documented, continually complicates and relocates the audience's point of view and gender sympathies. Our response to terror on the screen shifts from a desire to see innocent victims pursued and violently opened, to an insistence that their random deaths be revenged and the monster destroyed. While we may begin the film identifying with the monster (e.g., his male gaze) and his quest to punish the inane and carelessly lascivious behavior of the teens he hunts and kills, eventually our sympathies turn to his victims. We tire of his unimaginative stalkings, grow increasingly repulsed at his accumulated carnage, and come to appreciate and identify with the Final Girl, whose intelligence and stamina keep her alive: "Observers stress the readiness of the 'live' audience to switch sympathies midstream, siding now with the killer and now, and finally, with the Final Girl" (Clover 46).

These two paradigms of terror, Poe's interiorized gothic and the expansive gore of the contemporary slasher film, represent extremes of the horror aesthetic. Straddled between these two extremes we find a novel/ film such as *The Silence of the Lambs*, a text that, as we will see later, borrows heavily from both these Gothic strains. Poe is present in this narrative's blurring of the detective and horror genres, and in its psychological portraits of diseased psyches. *Silence* is, on the other hand, also a close kin to the slasher film with its strong emphasis upon the body, particularly female corporeality, and the unsettling level of visceral violence perpetrated against it. Whatever else he may be trying to become, as Clover reminds us, Buffalo Bill is the clear brother of Leatherface and Jason: a male desperate to disguise himself (and his self-hatred), a physical adult but spiritual child trapped in the lethal embrace of his mother, a tortured being obsessed with a sexuality that only serves to confuse and confound him (233).

Many people elect entertainment of a different variety from that found in the horror-thriller because they simply do not enjoy the sensation of experiencing psychological fear or physical fright. Correspondingly, the necessarily methodical assemblage of clues and information that allow the detective to solve the case sometimes alienates an audience attuned to more active plotlines. If we read detective fiction to experience vicariously the act of imposing order on chaos, we are conversely attracted to horror art because it puts us in a position where we are stimulated by forces out of control. Clearly, these represent the most fundamental responses to the two genres. But they are not the only reasons why detection and horror command such large popular followings and continue to produce important artistic contributions. Both genres, because they are forms of popular literature, reflect the fears and deepest concerns of the society from which they spring. They objectify the rage that Clarice Starling works so hard to manage.

Sociopolitical concerns are often exemplified in the specific types of transformations that occur in the horror tale. In the evolution of the horror monster, the creature comes to embody the fears and anxieties of the age he represents. Mr. Hyde, of *Dr. Jekyll and Mr. Hyde*, for example, can be interpreted as an extension of Victorian fears of the unrepressed psyche or of the fear of a retreat into prehistoric barbarism. Similarly, Jack Torrance is appropriately historicized as the contemporary American male of the late 1970s and early 1980s—obsessed with fame and the need for personal advancement—even if these must come at the expense of his family. Jame Gumb in *The Silence of the Lambs* tends to highlight postmodern culture's overemphasis on the body, and the symbolism that it represents as a signifier of gender consciousness that has reached the point of grotesque obsession. The nineteenth-century horror story tended to focus on a combination threat of deviant race, class, and gender; within contemporary horror, as Judith Halberstam has noted, the monster "tends to show clearly the markings of deviant sexualities and gendering, but less clearly the signs of class or race . . . . Monstrosity within contemporary horror seems to have stabilized into an amalgam of sex and gender" (4, 6).

A sociohistorical subtext can also be found in the detective story. For example, in *The Hound of the Baskervilles* the theme of atavism is brought up again and again, from the titles of Dr. Mortimer's articles on reversion and the question "Do We Progress?" to the reversion of Stapleton to his ancestor Sir Hugo Baskerville. Late nineteenth-century British society was unnerved by the dark side of evolution, whether it was possible to invert Darwin by returning to the animal state from which we had sprung. As *Dr. Jekyll and Mr. Hyde* embodied Victorian fears of the unrepressed psyche, so does *The Hound of the Baskervilles* embody the same society's fears of reverting back to a past animal ancestry. More contemporary detective writers express different concerns, as when Sara Paretsky relocates the motives for murder from the personal to the institutional to match the growing power and impersonality of the bureaucracy at the end of the twentieth century. Paretsky seems to attack the patriarchal structures of society as they are most obviously represented in corporate America. The "evil" in her tales appears to trickle down from the corporate hierarchy.

The point worth restating is that both horror and detection analyze, challenge, and sometimes subvert the value systems of any given cultural epoch; they ask us, however obliquely, to pay close attention to repressed communal insecurities. The halcyon years of science fiction, the 1950s, to cite just one case in point, frequently raised critical questions about science's pursuit of the atomic genie. The monsters in films such as *The Blob* or *The Thing* are always suggestive of a Faustian violation: society has sanctioned science to explore a side of nature that is best left undisturbed.

The detective story is not interested in the punishment of the murderer except in a symbolic way; it follows the criminal up to his arrest, which is considered punishment enough. The detective story doesn't care about how long the sentence is, nor whether the criminal is restored to society as a law-abiding citizen. It does not want to take the chance of the murderer getting off because of a clever lawyer or a lenient judge, nor does it aspire to some kind of moral conversion in the criminal. The detective story strives for knowledge, trying to know who did the murder, how she or he did it, and why.

What the detective searches for is the knowledge of the identity of the murderer and the revelation of that identity both to the reader and to the society in which the murder took place. According to Freud, discovery of the source of the rage is enough to cure the patient. The ultimate punishment of the murderer is to be publically identified and, in the case of the professional criminal, to be arrested. In that way, the reader can discover the sources of crime within his or her own heart and cast it out. Once this is done, the story can bump the murderer off in a symbolic way, such as having the murderer fall into the Grimpen Mire in *The Hound of the Baskervilles* or commit suicide by some appropriate means, as in *The Murder of Roger Ackroyd*. The detective story does not deal in legal proof, but in evidence that the reader will accept. Such cumulative evidence may not be suitable in a court of law, but it is acceptable in the court of the reader, satisfying her sense of justice and the urge to reimpose order.

The horror story seeks the reconfirmation of normalcy that existed at the beginning of the story. It attempts to overcome the monster either through some superhuman events or through the victim's powers of perseverance. In the horror films that Hollywood produced in the 1930s and 1940s, creatures such as Dracula, Frankenstein, and the Werewolf were destroyed by group action: a community banded together and exacted a revenge of the collective. In contemporary horror art, this large group action seldom occurs, perhaps mirroring a loss of righteous indignation as our response to the monster has become increasingly more ambivalent and any kind of national or community violence more suspect.

In many contemporary horror tales and films, the victim is usually female. And unlike the women who dominated Gothic romance novels in the eighteenth and nineteenth centuries, the contemporary female must survive the rampaging monster largely without hope of a male rescuer. As we will discuss in Chapter 4, in the past it was the future wife of the hero who got kidnapped by the monster and needed rescuing by the male hero. Perhaps reflecting the age of feminism—which is as much attacked as it is acknowledged in contemporary Gothicism—the heroine must rely on her own resources to survive. Her courage and wits are severely tested; they become her only means to combat and survive the threatening male monster.

The naming of the murderer and the overcoming of the monster leads through catharsis (as Auden describes it) to a world that erects a barrier against terror and murder. Catharsis is a release of emotions; the Other, the monster or the criminal, has been caught or destroyed. We are once more safe in our fictional worlds, which suggests, in a parallel way, that we are safe in our real ones. After all, the Other is overcome, we can now draw the covers up to our noses and sleep in peace and safety. In the horror story, the protagonist has survived, the monster has been overcome, even if only momentarily, and the world is once again comprehensible. The reader can presumably identify with the hero/heroine who finally kills the monster. Likewise, the detective has removed the murderer from society. Eighteenth-century Reason once again reigns: God's in his heaven, all's right with the world.

The typical conclusions for both these forms are a reaffirmation of the conservative morality around which popular forms coalesce. The horror story not only returns the world to the status quo, but uses the experience to show the final worth of the recently disrupted system. While the monster reveals the strains on that society, its rejection ultimately reaffirms the society itself. The detective story as well casts out the murderer to eliminate social disruption, at the same time revealing hidden secrets. These revelations allow society to cleanse itself and reestablish its equilibrium. The reader looks for a restoration of the status quo, either through the removal of the monster—be it human or supernatural—so that we can negotiate our own world, or through the removal of the murderer so that our world can proceed in safety. Both forms have a moral and religious base, as Auden's paradigm suggests. The detective story removes the criminal and solves the problems of identity (of the murderer) and fear (that somehow the murderer may be part of us). The horror story likewise teaches a lesson about transgressions into tabooed states: if the victim did not proceed into looking where he or she should not, then the monster might never have been released in the first place.

Poe's detective stories always end in this reimposed peace we have described: the ourang-outang is confined in a zoo, Minister D_____ falls to his political ruin. Poe's horror stories, on the other hand, are somewhat more problematic. Tales such as "The Black Cat" and "The Tell-Tale Heart" conclude in a manner that parallels the detective tale—i.e., the murderer is caught, incarcerated, and is no longer a threat to society. Other narratives are more equivocal in their resolutions. Many critical questions remain unanswered for those who would probe beyond the Gothic surfaces of tales such as "The Fall of the House of Usher": What is the "oppressive secret" between brother and sister that the narrator detects but cannot articulate? When Madeline emerges from the tomb, has she become a vampire in some form of the reanimated corpse? Is her purpose to save or doom her brother? And what kind of possible reimposition of the status quo is available to the narrator as he flees in mad horror from the dead siblings and crumbling Usher mansion?

Two final differences between these genres must be noted because of what they reveal about the narratological structures of each respective form. Detective fiction is normally narrated after its conclusion. The detective has survived and is once more in control. We are not surprised that Sue Grafton's novels are nominally in the form of reports given by Kinsey Millhone to somebody who is never identified (the client or reader is implied). The story has taken place in the past, and the tale is the story of the recovery of a story of a murder. The detective story's complex pattern of narration is one that distances the story and keeps it in the past. This approach allows a sense of narrative distance. After all, if the detective survives, the excitement of someone pulling a gun on her is vitiated by the prior knowledge that she escapes.

The horror story, on the other hand, is usually told in present tense; its effects are those that rear up at us suddenly from around the corner, from behind a bush. This is, of course, done deliberately, as placing the tale in the present serves to heighten the reader's anxieties and expectations. In Stephen King's 1988 novel, *IT*, for example, events from the past—both personal and historical—always bear an important relationship to the present. To do battle against It a second time, the adults in The Losers' Club must rediscover their connection to childhood, becoming, at least in their imaginations, children again. Thus, the past is a conduit to salvation (as well as terror) in this novel, but it is how the protagonists choose to utilize this collective past in the present that remains the essential narrative focus of *IT*.

What the children of Poe's fiction do is to make it possible for us to live in our world by providing us with ways of sublimating our collective rage into representations of evil's containment, in the detective tale, or by defeating those representatives, even if only temporarily, in the horror story. Poe provided patterns for two major branches of popular fiction which help us to understand the postmodern world. In fact, Mark Edmundson makes the argument in *Nightmare on Main Street* that the Gothic has supplied contemporary culture with its most pervasive metaphors, motifs, and recurring patterns of imagery. In their explorations of these two popular genres, detective fiction and horror literature, many writers today acknowledge Poe's paternity, but feel they have gone far beyond their father. Perhaps . . . but there are always those tell-tale signs of coming from the same family, of tics in the eye, of mouths shaped the same, of a certain droop to the mustache. No matter how far the children stray, they betray the traits of their ancestry.

Chapter 3
Poe's Victorian Disguises:
The Hound of the Baskervilles and
Dr. Jekyll and Mr. Hyde

> *Jekyll and Hyde* is a pre-Jungian fable, a vivid illustration of
> the Shadow side of a decent man, that aspect of our natures whose
> presence we all have to acknowledge. (Aldiss qtd. in Wolf 114)

Fifty years after Poe invented the detective story and provided the horror
tale with a level of psychological intensity to which it had not been pre-
viously subjected, Arthur Conan Doyle and Robert Louis Stevenson
adapted Poe's techniques in two of their most popular novels. Interestingly,
Sherlock Holmes depreciated Dupin to Watson in *A Study in Scarlet*: "In
my opinion, Dupin was a very inferior fellow. That trick of his of breaking in on his friends' [sic] thoughts with an apropos remark after a quar-
ter of an hour's silence is really very showy and superficial. He had some
analytical genius, no doubt; but he was by no means such a phenomenon
as Poe appeared to imagine" (25). His criticism notwithstanding, Holmes
modeled many of his investigative techniques after Poe's detective. In "A
Scandal in Bohemia," for instance, Holmes uses Watson to create the
diversion of a false fire in the same way that Dupin used the firing of an
unloaded musket in a crowd by a confederate to distract the Minister
D_____ in "The Purloined Letter."

Robert Louis Stevenson's investigation of the double or split personality is dependent upon Poe's initial treatment of this theme. Poe's
explanation of perversity helps us to understand why a thoroughly good
man, a well-respected doctor and honorable friend, would feel compelled
to turn himself into a monster. Moreover, Stevenson's novel takes place
in an environment that is decidedly Poe-like: from the symbolic interior
chambers of Jekyll's house and laboratory to the transformative energies
that occur to his main protagonist after dark.

Both Doyle's *The Hound of the Baskervilles* and Stevenson's *Dr. Jekyll
and Mr. Hyde* reflect Poe's world. Each portrays a patriarchal society in
which women are either victims or secondary to the privileged male power.
The only women in Poe's detective tales are victims: Mme. and Mlle.
L'Espanaye and Marie Roget. And with the exception of the vampire-lovers
we discussed in Chapter 1, the females in Poe's horror tales are also more
likely to be the objects of male violence. The only women in Stevenson's
novel are the small girl viciously trampled by Hyde, Jekyll's servants, and
women of the street. In Doyle's novel, women play a secondary role as
well, performing as servants or dependent on their husbands or lovers; the

narrative's main struggle is between Stapleton and Holmes. Poe's patriarchal world prevails in both of these Victorian tales, although the seeds of the growth in women's roles can be seen in such a tale as Doyle's "A Scandal in Bohemia."

Another of Poe's techniques that influenced Doyle and Stevenson is the creation of place as character. Baskerville Hall is located in the midst of the moor, a forbidding structure in a forbidding landscape. Within the moor is the Grimpen Mire, an area of quicksand that treacherously swallows up horses that gallop wild across the moor. The horses are sucked up, disappearing with a dreadful cry. The Mire waits for men. On the moor, within walking distance of the Mire, is Baskerville Hall, a habitation right out of the Gothic tale, formed by the same architect who constructed the infamous House of Usher: "The whole front was draped in ivy, with a patch clipped bare here and there where a window or coat of arms broke through the dark veil. From this central block rose twin towers, ancient, crenellated, and pierced with many loopholes" (375–76). This house is more solid than that of Usher since no crack runs up its side and it appears to be less sensitive to sibling reunions, but it is just as forbidding, maybe even more so because of its surroundings. The city of London has given way to the country of Dartmoor.

Just as the Baskerville mansion and the Grimpen Mire signal the darkest inclinations at work in Doyle's novel (indeed, Stapleton plots his nefarious schemes from within the Mire where the demonic hound is also found), physical settings in *Dr. Jekyll and Mr. Hyde* highlight the dual nature of the narrative's protagonist. The address where both Jekyll and Hyde reside is the same, yet the chambers within the building itself mirror the personality split that gives birth to Hyde. The part of the house where Jekyll resides features all the physical comforts and civilized amenities that might be associated with one of London's most respected physicians: "This hall, in which he was now left alone, was a pet fancy of his friend the doctor's; and Utterson himself was wont to speak of it as the pleasantest room in London" (53). On the other hand, the area that Hyde inhabits is located in the back of the house, behind Jekyll's quarters. It is secreted, much like Hyde himself, from the places in which Jekyll conducts his business, personal as well as professional. Jekyll's front door opens to one of the most elegant streets in London; the door that Hyde uses "equipped with neither bell nor knocker, was blistered and distained" (39). On Hyde's side of the building we find the darker impulses of the human psyche: men conducting strange errands at three in the morning, dubious activities that are cloaked in secrecy, and society's own unacknowledged denizens—tramps and delinquent children forever lost, geographically and spiritually.

Jekyll's hall and Hyde's laboratory, Jekyll's front door and Hyde's rear entry, Jekyll's brightly-lit parlor filled with colleagues and friends and

Hyde's shadowy isolation—all are part of the same building—as Hyde is the brooding "Juggernaut" (40) contained within the placid doctor. As the narrators of Poe's horror tales house an internal dualism that make them both criminal and victim to the acts they perpetrate, the two sides of Jekyll are represented in the man of science and the creature that science created. Vladimir Nabokov was first to point out that Hyde can no more be separated from Jekyll than the subconscious part of the mind can be disconnected from the conscious. Both share an intimacy that is, like the geography of place in Stevenson's novel, housed within a single entity. And as the subconscious part of the psyche exists to haunt the conscious mind, Hyde is that part of Jekyll.

Stevenson wrote a novel about doors; doors that preserve secrets, and doors that betray them. The nature of doors is to protect the interiors that are located behind them, to allow entry as well as to forbid it (Wolf 54). The doors that appear in *Dr. Jekyll and Mr. Hyde* are physical, as we have seen, but they are also metaphorical, as in the frequent dream that Utterson is said to experience early in the novel. He locates himself in Jekyll's bedroom, watching his friend sleep, when Hyde appears as a dual nightmare intruding into this dream-within-a-dream, crossing through the doors of both bedroom and psyche: "[Utterson] would see a room in a rich house, where his friend lay asleep, dreaming and smiling at his dreams; and then the door of that room would be opened, the curtains of the bed plucked apart, the sleeper recalled, and lo! there would stand by his side a figure to whom power was given, and even at that dead hour, he must rise and do its bidding" (48). This dream sequence specifically links Mr. Hyde with the unconscious mind and the fact that its power is so great that the conscious mind—"the sleeper recalled"—is a prisoner to its demands, forced to "rise and do its bidding." But Hyde appears to haunt not only the darkest recesses of Jekyll's mind, but violates the threshold of Utterson's as well.

Throughout this novel doors are constantly being forced open to reveal the illicit and horrific contents they hide. "The Last Night" section, for example, requires Utterson and Poole to break down the door to Jekyll's laboratory. Once inside, the only trace of Henry Jekyll that remains is his final act of suicide: forced to kill the opposing sides of his psyche because Hyde had destroyed the balance. In the symbolism of Utterson's dream, Hyde is again the dominant figure, as he is throughout his interactions with Jekyll, violating private domestic thresholds—the bed curtains as well as bedroom door—to interrupt the doctor's happy dreams and sense of security. Stevenson posits in this scene (and will extend this argument through the novel's spontaneous and unprovoked recollections that transform Jekyll into Hyde with greater frequency and without warning) that once the "door" separating the unconscious from the conscious is opened, it becomes difficult, if not impossible, to close it again. The deceptive

Jekyll conceals Hyde within himself and is confident that he can become Jekyll whenever he wants, a supreme example of the doctor's scientific hubris. But Hyde cannot be eliminated from Jekyll; there are at least two occasions in the narrative where Jekyll is transformed into Hyde unexpectedly. While the evil of Hyde can exist alone, the social Jekyll cannot exist without the atavistic Hyde. Indeed, Stevenson's story goes so far as to argue that the unconscious and irrational side of humankind is just as powerful (and perhaps more so once it is unleashed) than our rational and conscious impulses. Once the beast is set free, it is extremely difficult to cage him again. Thus, Jekyll discovers that he cannot keep Hyde contained in his laboratory bottles.

Stevenson's and Doyle's novels, published at the end of the nineteenth century, can be considered mirror images of each other because they deal with similar themes and techniques. But this is not surprising, considering their mutual source in the writings of Poe. Each novel often relies upon the characteristics of its sibling. *Dr. Jekyll and Mr. Hyde* is a horror story which tries to use the rational techniques of the detective story; *Baskervilles* is a detective story haunted by the ghost story. Daniel Sheridan, in "Later Victorian Ghost Stories: The Literature of Belief," characterizes the different emphasis of both tales: there are "tales of the supernatural, like *The Hound of the Baskervilles*, in which the ghost is explained away in natural terms; and tales of the pure supernatural, in which the ghost turns out to be indeed supernatural" (35). While the narrative design of *Jekyll* suggests a rational tale of science run amok, the fact that Jekyll is transformed physically into a monstrous being pushes the implications of internal dissonance found in Poe's "William Wilson" to its supernatural extreme. Stevenson and Doyle try to come to grips with man's place in a shifting universe, and the unstable quality of that universe is what causes the novels themselves to shift beneath our feet. Their respective narratives face some of the same problems also encountered by Poe: how to deal with the fear at the center of life when life itself appears out of control; how to re-establish that control or adapt to the new circumstances that emerge to fill the vacuum. Both novels take place in the battle ground between hostile Apollonian and Dionysian forces (Nietzsche 556), and while each acknowledges the power of the other, in the end, *Jekyll* is clearly a tale of supernatural horror while *Baskervilles* subverts the supernatural in re-establishing the rational dominance of the detective.

The Hound of the Baskervilles begins with a declaration by Sherlock Holmes that if "'we are dealing with forces outside the ordinary laws of Nature, there is an end of our investigation. But we are bound to exhaust all other hypotheses before falling back on this one'" (358). Holmes does not deny the existence of the supernatural, just our abilities to deal with it. We must confront and exhaust all other possibilities within the rational realm. In fact, Holmes is willing to—nay, asserts that he *must*—abandon the case if it contains a supernatural thread. This observation is ironic in that the supernatural thread was suggested by Dr. Mortimer, a man of science whose specialty is both banal and scientific: the measurement of skulls. Mortimer's writings include "Is Disease a Reversion?" "Some Freaks of Atavism," and "Do We Progress?" (345). Holmes's world is one of probability and rationality, as when he finds the source of the anonymous note warning Sir Henry away from London and when he tries to determine the identity of the man in the cab by sending a telegram to Barrymore at Baskerville Hall to eliminate him as one of the suspects. He is reluctant to admit supernatural causes, even though in the Baskerville case there seems to be a weight of supernatural evidence.

In a similar way, none of Jekyll's male cronies is willing to believe in the possibility that Hyde and Jekyll are one and the same. All of Stevenson's male characters are rational men; thus, in their eyes, Jekyll's misappropriation of scientific principles becomes all the more shocking and contemptible. Like Hawthorne's Aylmer in the story "The Birthmark," Jekyll's moment of scientific triumph is also his greatest moment of failure. When confronted with things that seem to be beyond the ken of science or experience, either Utterson or the police use well-known detective procedures to try to explain the inexplicable. In searching for clues after the murder of Sir Danvers Carew, an inspector finds the charred end of a cheque book. "'You may depend upon it, sir' [the inspector] told Mr. Utterson 'I have him in my hand. He must have lost his head, or he would never have . . . burned the cheque book. Why, money's life to the man. We have nothing to do but wait for him at the bank, and get out the handbills'" (64). This conclusion is worthy of a hard-boiled American detective, but, alas, it does not work. In a similar way, Utterson tries to explain to Poole, Jekyll's butler, why Jekyll wears a mask. "'These are all very strange circumstances, . . . but I think I begin to see daylight. Your master, Poole, is plainly seized with one of those maladies that both torture and deform the sufferer; hence, for aught I know, the alteration of his voice; hence, the mask and the avoidance of his friends; hence, his eagerness to find the drug, by means of which the poor soul retains some hope of ultimate recovery'" (84–85).

Both novels are concerned with disguises, secrets, hidden personalities, and the problems of what we carry inside ourselves. Mrs. Stapleton is disguised as Stapleton's sister. Stapleton himself pretends to be Laura Lyons' suitor in order to use her to get rid of Sir Charles. Stapleton himself is really a Baskerville, hoping to inherit the fortune when his true identity is revealed. As a friend and neighbor of Sir Henry, Stapleton conceals the evil hidden inside himself and symbolized by the Grimpen Mire.

In Stevenson's text, Jekyll and his cronies hide their emotionalism, their passions, and their sexual energies under their professionalism and bourgeois shields of respectability. At the core of Jekyll's group there is an egotism—a prideful superiority—that Hyde, the most selfish and imperious of them all, embodies. It is thus ironic that all of these men refuse to acknowledge consciously their potential identification with Hyde. Indeed, on several occasions Jekyll's cronies appear willing to engage morally, if not legally, compromising actions to insulate Hyde's violent behavior and thereby preserve Dr. Jekyll's independence. For example, it is a very curious breakfast party, including Enfield, the trampled girl's father, and the doctor, who in the novel's opening scene await the bank to open so that Hyde can essentially buy his way out of trouble. There is a subtle collusion at work among all these men who profess to hate Hyde and are repulsed by his awful trampling of the girl. Yet in this scene and in others throughout the text, Hyde is protected by Jekyll's friends and colleagues, the latter in turn believing that they are somehow also protecting Dr. Jekyll. The monster's actions throughout the novel underscore the fact that affluent single men have always possessed the freedom to engage in behavior of their own choosing, and then retreat behind a safe veneer of proper conduct. The real horror of this novel is not found only in Jekyll's misuse of science, but in the sobering possibility that a powder compound may not necessarily be required to summon the Hyde that lurks within each of us.

A Victorian context aids in understanding the issues present within both these narratives. Victorian readers were concerned with Darwinism. Those who denied the idea of the descent of man, who felt that humans had issued fully formed from the hand of God, were threatened by the new theories. They felt beleaguered by the attacks of scientists, those who had "proof" of the non-existence of God. They denied that man and monkey were related, but many of their most vehement denials suggest an uncomfortable feeling that there were too many parallels between the two species to be ignored. Those who followed Darwin felt that humans had soared high above their beginnings, taking a long journey from their animal beginnings to their present exalted status. The Romantic sensibility world welcomed Darwin's thesis of an inextricable bond between the natural and human worlds. Victorians, on the other hand, had a profound distaste for the bizarre and the fantastic; for them, the link between human and ape was cause for cultural stress rather than celebration. Jekyll and Hyde came to represent for the Victorian imagination the essential threshold figure between the human and animal realms. This fear of atavism was also a favorite topic for Doyle's Dr. Mortimer, of evincing within humans characteristics which indicate a throwback to their animal natures. People of England prided "themselves on a Britain that seemed to be progressing to ever-new heights [but] secretly feared something below the surface" (Keating 21). They feared their own inner beings might revert to savagery in some form of atavism, "the recurrence of primitive characteristics from the remote past" (21). They feared "the violence within" (22), that propensity toward savagery that civilization was intended to have brought them beyond. They looked with horror at the idea of sliding back down the chute, as in the children's game of Chutes and Ladders, of somehow reverting inexorably to their animal natures. Dr. Watson incites this Victorian paranoia in his atavistic description of caves of prehistoric dwellers on the moor in one of his letters to Holmes: "When you are once out upon [the moor] you have left all traces of modern England behind you, but on the other hand you are conscious everywhere of the homes and the work of the prehistoric people . . . . As you look at their grey stone huts against the scarred hill-sides you leave your own age behind you, and if you were to see a skin-clad, hairy man crawl out from the low door, fitting a flint-tipped arrow on to the string of his bow, you would feel that his presence there was more natural than your own" (385). Essentially, Stevenson's and Doyle's novels prey upon Victorian anxieties about their place in the evolution of the species. These texts suggest that humankind's nature may have more in common with the apes than with the angels.

The reactions to this fear of atavism not only pervaded the lecture circuit and the major journals of the time, but also the popular literature. Both *The Hound of the Baskervilles* and *Dr. Jekyll and Mr. Hyde* have, as their major impetus, a reaction to these social fears. Doyle's Dr. Mortimer, obsessed with this concept of atavism, asks, "Do We Progress?" Looking at the evidence, it might seem that if the answer is an affirmative, it is put forth without much confidence.

Each novel presents characteristics of evolutionary throwback in the small stature of regressive beings: Selden, the convict, in Doyle; and Hyde in Stevenson. Both these men are of smaller stature than normal, as if man, on his pathway to progress, had grown taller (a prejudice which still exists in our own society which gives tall men a pre-eminent place and brushes aside those of a "lower" stature). Selden is described in terms of an animal: a "terrible animal face," "small, cunning eyes . . . like a crafty and savage animal" (399). When he is discovered, Selden curses and hurls a rock (a primitive weapon) at Dr. Watson and Sir Henry Baskerville. Watson catches sight of "his short, squat, strongly-built figure" which rapidly disappears as he easily outruns his more civilized human pursuers (400). Selden's animal qualities culminate in his animal speed and the savagery of his actions, as well as the savagery of his crimes.

Hyde, Jekyll's inner regressive being, is described by Enfield as being "deformed somewhere," (43) although Enfield cannot specify what the deformity is. The only consistent details are his small stature and grotesque appearance. "Little" is the very first word that Enfield uses in describing Hyde (40), and he goes on to say that he first observed Hyde "slumping along eastward" (40) which suggests the latter's warped and deformed status. Utterson recalls him as "pale and dwarfish . . . he had a displeasing smile, he had borne himself . . . with a sort of murderous mixture of timidity and boldness . . . but not all of these together could explain the hitherto unknown disgust, loathing and fear" (52) which Hyde inspired. Hyde's hand was of a "dusky pallor and thickly shaded with a swart growth of hair" (112). While other specific details are missing, Hyde fills the London citizenry with a sense of loathing in his bestial appearance. He snarls, he growls, he acts the animal to Jekyll's facade of noble humanity.

Both Selden and Hyde are projections of the evil which resides, hidden, within society. For Doyle, these regressions are illustrated in three figures: the convict, the hound, and the criminal Stapleton. Selden's actions are not only illegal (he is known as the "Notting Hill murderer") but horrible. His crimes were marked with "peculiar ferocity" and "wanton brutality" (375). He is cut off from almost all human intercourse. His only connection is with his sister, Mrs. Barrymore, who supplies him with food, clothing, and a chance to flee the country. Her kindness comes from her memories of childhood, when she acted the older sister. It is this memory which moves her, not a commitment to protecting the perpetrator of such evil crimes.

The dog itself is further evidence of a throwback, a reversion to the spectral hound that tore out the throat of Sir Hugo. The hound has its origins in the ghost stories of the Victorian era. If Doyle were creating one of those tales, the beast would have been a real ghost, wreaking its vengeance on the descendents of the Baskerville lineage. Many ghost tales would have found the hound triumphant in destroying all the remnants of the family. But this is a detective tale, not a ghost story, and nothing is allowed to exist which cannot be scientifically explained. Thus, it is left for science to discredit the supernatural and return the narrative to the natural—a movement that is in opposition to the supernatural transformation that occurs to Dr. Jekyll. But even though science and the rational triumph in Doyle (the hound is shot), Sir Henry Baskerville is almost killed in the obscuring fog and the howls of the hound continue to resonate even after the creature is dead. Indeed, the image of this dog aggressively bearing down upon its human prey dominates the reader's memory of this book.

Stapleton is himself a throwback: his face sprang out of Sir Hugo's portrait. Holmes reveals to Watson that the eighteenth-century portrait of Sir Hugo could have been done of Stapleton. Stapleton is a descendent of the evil branch of the Baskerville family (a standard Gothic trope), carrying its bad blood in an undiluted stream from the wrong side of the family. His evil nature is illustrated in his beating of his wife, in his betrayal of Laura Lyons, in the way he uses fear of the past to kill Sir Charles, and in his association with the Grimpen Mire. As Selden is associated with the lonely and hilly moor, his evil nature illustrated in its gloomy isolation, so is Stapleton associated with the quicksands of the Mire, its swallowing up of wild horses, and its deceptive bearing concealing the evil under its placid skin of sand. Stapleton is at home in this inhospitable place, the only one capable of negotiating around this landscape of evil, maintaining his reign of fear by keeping the hound free of discovery in the center of the Mire.

One of the more sobering elements in each of these novels concerns the fact that both Stevenson and Doyle probed the darker sides of human nature. Stapleton and Seldon are Doyle's degenerate men, fallen beings who have lost touch with the affirmative virtues of society and morality that the detective represents and seeks to uphold. In *Jekyll and Hyde*, Dr. Jekyll manages to refrain from using the powder that summons Hyde for more than a two-month period. As a consequence, he informs us proudly that he "enjoyed the compensations of an approving conscience" (115). But this novel has often been interpreted as a study in substance abuse addiction because none of the satisfaction that Jekyll attains in practicing abstinence—from a return to the social world of friends and charitable work to the security of his professional reputation—is sufficient to deter him from the blood rush that he gains in becoming Hyde: "I began to be tortured with throes and longings, as of Hyde struggling after freedom; and at last, in an hour of moral weakness, I once again compounded and swallowed the transforming draught" (115). Jekyll comprehends fully that becoming Hyde is a dangerous and morally dubious act, a risk to everything he values most in his life. But Stevenson has provided us with yet another illustration of Poe's Imp of the Perverse: Jekyll is drawn to self-destructive behavior in spite of the consequences; in fact, the risk involved only seems to heighten his need for the experience.

Jekyll is the only one who is in possession of the truth about Mr. Hyde. In place of Holmes's employment of science as an instrument for man's progress and advancement, Jekyll reverts to using science as a means of uncovering man's deathless cycle of sin. Stevenson's tale offers a disintegrating vision of life through chemistry, while Doyle would remind us that life is only bearable when it is under the control of reason. Like Holmes, Jekyll trusts implicitly in his science and his powers of self-discipline, believing that he can regulate his journey into the heart of darkness. But Mr. Hyde proves otherwise: that Darwin's theories of our close intimacy with the bestial world more than justify Victorian discomfort, and we deny the power of this connection at great risk. If Holmes is a constant reminder of the Enlightenment's view of reason as a guiding force to regulating human behavior, Jekyll into Hyde suggests the opposite: that reason is an inadequate barrier to the perversity inherent in human nature.

These novels resemble each other in other important ways. Both are told through the eyes of a solid Englishman, unpoetic, rational, and sensible. Both these narrators are derived from Poe's narrator in the Dupin tales. Watson, who tells the Holmes tale through memory, letters, and diaries, is all common sense. His detection, when Holmes is not on the scene, is expert and sharp. Watson acts quickly and decisively, spying on Mrs. Barrymore, pursuing Selden over the moor, interviewing Laura Lyons. When Holmes is there, Watson willingly assumes a more diminutive status, taking orders from Holmes, depending on him for conclusions, action, and decisions. In other words, Watson is a conventionally secondary narrator except when, in the absence of Holmes, he becomes the only one on the field. Watson's values are those of his audience: he is kindly, protective of women, in touch with his emotions, living up to a code of honor. He is prosy, except for certain moments, such as in his description of the prehistoric dwellers on the moor.

In contrast, one of Stevenson's central narrators, Utterson, is a man with even less of the softer passions. Watson is married and has some social and home life. Utterson's social life consists solely of Sunday walks with his friend Enfield; his close friends seem to be only those men whom he knew in school, and he has maintained contact with only a few of them. His social relations seem to be repressed, and his only emotion is that of shock at actions that violate the sensibilities of the British male. His social life appears to revolve around the three friends of whom we are aware: Enfield, Lanyon, and Jekyll. Perhaps the intimacy of this social circle deepens the loss when something tragic happens to one of its members. Utterson experiences the loss of Lanyon and Jekyll, and it is perhaps as a result of their deaths that we find Utterson mute at the end of the novel. Lanyon may die for the same reason that Utterson goes mute: they both sense this dark bond with Hyde. As we traced earlier in this chapter, Hyde's presence haunts Utterson's dreamscape; similarly, Hyde's existence shakes Lanyon's complacent theories on science and society to such a degree that he does not recover.

The other similarity that ties these two texts is their layered narratives. *Baskerville* is told directly through Watson, beginning the tale when he enters 221B Baker Street. But the novel soon changes to excerpts from Watson's diaries (supposedly told in reflection over recent events) and from letters (even more of a present-time narrative device). Through these various mirrors of time, Watson is able to involve us more and more in the tale until the end, when he and Holmes reflect on the newly concluded case. The story begins in familiar surroundings, the apartment shared by Watson and Holmes, moves into the exciting present, then returns to the reflections of the conclusion. This sense of stylistic closure is characteristic of the detective novel.

Dr. Jekyll and Mr. Hyde's narrative is told through the point of view of Utterson, even in the first chapter when Enfield relates the story of his first meeting with Hyde. Utterson sees puzzling clues, all of which he tries to confront with his own logical, detective-like mind. At the end, though, when the narrative leaves the matter-of-fact world of Utterson, it moves into two letters, one from Lanyon, the other from Jekyll, which detail the most fantastic parts of the narrative. By moving the last two chapters into the words of two other speakers, Stevenson leaves the rational world of the detective novel behind and advances into the world of the suprarational; our last anchor to reality is that of the man—Utterson—who reads these letters and apparently gives them credence. The reader's horrified response is all the greater for being refracted through the understanding of Utterson, as our involvement in *Baskervilles* is enhanced by having the story told through the sensibilities of Watson. It is not accidental that there are so many doctors involved in both these stories; their number helps with narrative verisimilitude. Moreover, Stevenson's long history of grave illness would suggest that especially in his case the occupation of physician was held with most profound respect and trust.

Each of these narratives questions basic conceptions of progress. In *The Hound of the Baskervilles* Sir Henry goes on a long voyage for the recovery of his shattered nerves (440) to regain strength enough to face the world again. His earlier scientific faith in the Swan and Edison generator (376), which would be used to illuminate the darkness of Baskerville Hall, is ultimately undermined by the eternal fog of the moor. Similarly, Utterson's and Lanyon's worlds of self-control and rationality crumble in the face of testimony that describes persuasively the result of Gothic science used to open doors that contain forbidden knowledge. Holmes provides *Baskervilles* with an ultimate return to the security of a rational universe where the scientific method explains away the mysteries of the apparently inexplicable. No such complacency, however, is available in Stevenson's novel. The Jekyll/Hyde suicide is the final image the reader takes away from the experience of entering into this nightmare. One can only imagine that Utterson's future Sunday walks will steer clear of Jekyll's neighborhood. The novel's implications are sobering reminders that every human mind contains realms its owner explores with the assistance of neither guide nor map, and that sometimes the choice to explore these worlds is a tragic and one-way journey that can never be exculpated.

Chapter 4

Poe Feminized: Daughters of Fear and Detection

Who has *not* been influenced by Poe?—however obliquely, indirectly; however the influence, absorbed in adolescence or even in childhood, would seem to be far behind us. (Oates, *Haunted* 305)

Women have been writing Gothic and detective fiction from the inception of each respective genre; they either have written adopting the patriarchal viewpoint of their own times or have tried to subvert those values in some disguised manner. The most popular detective writer, regardless of gender, Agatha Christie, adopted the male point of view in her Hercule Poirot tales as told by Captain Hastings. Her female detectives, such as Miss Marple, for all their sympathy and wisdom, are marginalized, removed from the center of power. Christie's adoption of the gendered assumptions of her time worked against the subversive nature of women's writing. Another of the great female detective writers, Dorothy L. Sayers, did not fare much better in the arena of innovative gender politics. Sayers placed Lord Peter Wimsey at the center of her novels, even those about Harriet Vane. *Gaudy Night*, which focuses on the question of the proper role of women in society, is a good case in point as it shows Vane accepting Wimsey's marriage proposal only under the condition that the two remain equal in their relationship. Vane may accept Wimsey's proposal, but it is really Lord Peter who allows her to be herself.

Throughout the detective genre, and sometimes even in those instances where the author is a female, it is possible to argue that male values have dominated: males were to be respected, society's patriarchal values reinforced, women were relegated to their secondary roles as wives and mothers. Until work shaped most recently by feminism which, as we shall see, has helped reconfigure both the Gothic and detective tale, these values remained unquestioned. The Gothic heroine, as much a presence in the detective genre as she was a staple in the horror tale, has traditionally occupied the role of a potential victim to be rescued and protected by men. As Linda Williams points out, "In classic horror [and detective fiction], the woman encountered a monster whose deformed features suggested a distorted mirror-reflection of her own putative lack in the eyes of the patriarchy" (25). While both genres might question the social construction that placed women in such restrictive and vulnerable roles, neither horror nor detection was quick to offer plausible alternatives; in fact, there has always been a particular level of titillation that attends the plight and rescue of the besieged heroine, whether she is troubled by monster or criminal. In short, women were to be avenged by good men, found either in the role of the detective or the ever-dedicated husband/husband-to-be; their innocence brought to light; their honor satisfied. To paraphrase Pope, detective and horror fiction have traditionally accepted the status quo: whatever is, is as it should be.

Prior to the advent of modern feminism, women's roles in the Gothic and detective genres were typically that of Mrs. Barrymore in *The Hound of the Baskervilles*: she supplies cleaning and other services as a maid. Her brother, the criminal Selden, plays upon her sympathies; she remembers him only as "the little curly-headed boy that I had nursed and played with, as an elder sister would" (397). Laura Lyons, who defied her father Frankland to marry an unworthy man, is caught in a marital tangle: Lyons can still assert his legal powers and force his wife to live with him, even against her will (410). Her social role is defined by patriarchal privilege exclusive to either father or husband; unable to get along with either, she turns to another man, Sir Charles Baskerville, for help. As a female she has no resources of her own, and her very dependency allows her to be used by Stapleton to carry out Sir Charles's murder. Mrs. Stapleton is bound by her role as wife and the forces of love and fear which Stapleton wields over her. Only the news "that she had a rival in his love" (445) turns her marital fidelity into hatred and moves her to thoughts of betrayal. She is brought to an active position over her own life only when her affections become embittered. But even then, her change is initially occasioned by a male choice: the abandonment of a husband's responsibilities which, in turn, cause his wife to reconsider her role.

Women in Poe, as in most Gothic tales, are often victims. Madeleine Usher, the Lady Rowena Trevanion, Morella, Berenice, the wife in "The Black Cat," all die or are prematurely buried, victims of brother, lover, husband. As we traced in Chapter 1, some women (Ligeia, Morella, Madeline Usher) exert power over their tormentors, but they do so at the cost of their own lives. Ligeia returns to torture her lover; Madeline Usher is buried alive by her brother, Roderick, who knows she is not dead, and she exacts a terrible vengeance which results in both their deaths. Even in their deathly power, these women are victims. In the detective tales, Mme. and Mlle. L'Espanaye, as well as Marie Roget, are murdered, and the Queen's reputation and career are given over to the power of Minister D_____.

Poe changed the Gothic tale by telling the tale from the point of view of the monster: vengeful Montressor, the nocturnal murderer in "The Tell-Tale Heart," the tortured and tormenting narrator in "The Black Cat." In his development of the detective story, Poe centered his attention not on the voice of the narrator, but rather on the structure of the narration itself, producing a new form in telling the story backwards and, more importantly, in his manipulation of point of view (Panek, *Introduction*, 32). It is thus through this reconfiguration in development of point of view that both Gothic and detective fictions show their narratological descent from Poe.

When the feminist movement gathered momentum in the 1970s, it feminized the Gothic and the detective story. In the latter, it introduced women detectives who are neither superannuated (like Miss Marple) nor bubble-headed (Nora Charles). They become the equivalent of the male detectives, often, at first, adopting the hard-boiled techniques of the American detective story and feminizing or altering their techniques. They were, according to Marilyn Stasio, less violent and more sympathetic than the male private investigators, compassionate and more emotional. They were also no longer shackled by the "marriage plot," in which the heroine's "status as a marriageable woman" is at odds with her career (Klein 37). Earlier women detectives were portrayed as successful in the one (she married and abandoned detection) or the other (she remained a detective, spurning the offers of marriage for her career). Even in a modern novel, such as Sara Paretsky's *Bitter Medicine*, the detective, Warshawski, is advised by Sergio, a gang leader: "'you're not any better off than when I saw you last, Warshawski. I hear you're still driving a beater, still living by yourself. You should get married, Warshawski. Settle down'" (53). And, in threatening her and then cutting her face, Sergio carefully keeps the cut to the side, saying, "'I don't want to ruin you in case you ever get a man'" (56). To add insult to injury, the physician who sews up Warshawski's face gives the following prognosis: "'Your boyfriend may see a faint line when he kisses you, but if he's that close he probably won't be looking.'" "Sexist asshole," thinks Warshawski, but she doesn't say it aloud because one doesn't bite "the hand that sews you"; nevertheless, she herself is worried about the scar (61). Even Kinsey Millhone, Sue Grafton's detective who is even less concerned with her appearance, feels the need for a steady man on whom she can lean: Robert Dietz appears in *"A" Is for Alibi, "G" Is for Gumshoe,* and *"J" Is for Judgment* and serves as her protector and lover.

Women detectives conceive of reality in different terms than their male counterparts. Although she is often disruptive in her methods, Warshawski describes her actions as a detective in mildly feminine terms: "My theory of detection resembles Julia Child's approach to cooking: Grab a lot of ingredients from the shelves, put them in a pot and stir, and see what happens" (Klein 213). Millhone makes the food connection when viewing dead bodies; she uses the reference as a way of relieving tension in the particularly macabre world of detective fiction. She describes part of an autopsy when the pathologist is inventorying the inner organs: "Well, let's see. There's a heart. Liver. Lung. Spleen. Gall bladder . . . I didn't think I'd ever look at stew meat in quite the same way." She later describes a corpse she is searching for a murder weapon: "He was surprisingly light and cold to the touch, about the consistency of a package of raw chicken breasts just out of the fridge" (Schaffer 319). Even such a devoted cook as Robert B. Parker's Spenser would not use food or cooking in this particular way.

But what we are most interested in pursuing here, particularly within the writings of Paretsky and Grafton, is not only how women detective writers have changed the form and written some of the most interesting fiction of the last fifteen years, but also what they have inherited from Poe. Poe's tales possess a sexual subtext that many critics have uncovered in such stories as "Ligeia," "Berenice," and "The Fall of the House of Usher." More often than not, Poe combines the sexual urge with violent energies, so that the two become almost indistinguishable. In "Berenice," for example, the narrator's treatment of women stands out as one of Poe's most shocking and repulsive descriptions of masculine aggressiveness. Obsessed with Berenice's mouth and teeth, the narrator's erotic fascination increases in proportion to the pain the woman experiences as she is ravaged first by epilepsy and then the narrator's rape of her mouth, pulling teeth from her jaw even as her screams protest against the thirty-two-step oral extraction. A Freudian reading of this tale sees the narrator's violent desecration of Berenice's mouth as a vaginal violation and assault against the mother in the narrator's symbolic mutilation of the entrance to the womb.

Throughout the detective genre, Poe's negative attitude toward both women and sexuality appears in a variety of texts. S.S. Van Dine has gone so far to insist in Rule 3 of the "Twenty Rules for Writing Detective Stories" that "There must be no love interest" (Haycroft, *Art* 189). In the tradition of the hardboiled detective tale, the same destructive sexual energy we have seen at work in Poe is almost exclusively female; like Morella and Ligeia, there is a fatal attractiveness to the *femmes fatales* of the hard-boiled genre. Primarily created by male authors, who have been strongly influenced by a Hemingwayesque distrust of women in general, hard-boiled detectives face killers who are often female, and these women employ their beauty and sexuality in manipulative and predatory fashions.

Sam Spade, in *The Maltese Falcon*, finds his killer in Brigid O'Shaughnessy while Philip Marlowe, in *The Big Sleep*, find his in Carmen Sternwood. When we turn to recent women detective writers, on the other hand, these masculine constructions of women are often undermined. Warshawski and Millhone are much less puritanical and more open to sexual experiences without the punishments that go along with them. Spade makes quite clear why he can't go with O'Shaughnessy; he could never trust her and she might betray him at any time. Warshawski likewise protects herself by avoiding commitment to her sexual partner, and the casualness of her approach is part of the new attitude of female writers to sex.

Both before and after Poe, the literature of terror has remained fascinated with elements of a dark sexuality, particularly the aberrant sexuality of incest, rape, violence, necrophilia, vampirism, bondage, and sado-masochism. The Gothic heroine is usually cast as the object of pursuit by the Gothic villain, the latter psychosexually obsessed with one or more of these perverse sexual acts. In the detective tale, when such aberrant behavior manifests itself, it is typically confined to the criminal, and helps to define the perversity of his nature. The male detective, in contrast, remains either asexual (e.g., Dupin and Holmes) or manifests his essential moral decency and core stability in the normalcy of his sex drive (e.g., Steve Carella's genuine appreciation for the physical relationship he shares with his wife, Teddy, in Ed McBain's Eighty-Seventh Precinct series).

The contemporary women detective novelists we are interested in examining in this chapter exhibit a unique attitude toward their female protagonists' sexuality. Although many female detective authors will sometimes re-employ the Gothic's distinct portrayal of women under siege, these writers are also interested in moving their women characters beyond the role of mere victim, most notably when it comes to the issue of gender relationships. Like many contemporary feminist writers, Sara Paretsky and Sue Grafton wish to create complex and realistic women characters whose attitudes toward sex are as multidimensional as the other aspects of their lives.

Warshawski's affair with Peter Burgoyne, the physician from Friendship Hospital who seduces her to find out what she knows in the novel *Bitter Medicine*, is not highly charged; it seems more a matter of opportunity than of desire on her part. The low voltage of the relationship seems to be geared to the fact that, not only is Peter part of the institution that is at the center of evil of this novel, but he is pushed out of the center by Alan Humphries. Burgoyne's suicide undermines the novel's sense of closure: we want to punish Humphries rather than Burgoyne. Millhone's more passionate nature is shown in her attraction to Charlie Scorsoni, who makes her feel safe and warm when they have sex. When she discovers he is a murderer and he hunts her with a knife, however, she overcomes her attraction and deftly resolves her ambivalence, shooting him when he finds her hiding in a dumpster.

In *"G" Is for Gumshoe*, Kinsey Millhone pursues the mystery of what happened to Irene Gersh's mother while she herself is pursued by a killer hired by Tyrone Patty. Millhone abruptly finds herself in the role of the potential victim, protected by Dietz but pursued by Mark Messinger. Like the Gothic heroine, she is unwittingly attracted to her pursuer. When Messinger sets her up by posing as a UPS man, she responds both to his violence as well as to his sexuality:

The UPS man was coming up the walk behind us. He was smiling at me and I felt myself smile automatically in response. He was a big man, muscular, clean-shaven, with blond curly hair, stark blue eyes in a tan face, full mouth curving into dimpled cheeks. I thought I must know him because he seemed glad to see me, his eyes soft, the look on his face both sensual and warm. He moved nearer, bending toward me, almost as if he meant to kiss me. He was so close I registered the heady bouquet of his personal scent: gunpowder, Aqua Velva after-shave, and a whiff of Juicy Fruit chewing gum. I felt myself drawing back, perplexed. Behind me, wood snapped like a tree being cracked by lightning. I could see his face suffuse with heat, like a lover at the moment of his climax. (167)

Here we find Millhone trapped in the role of the Gothic maiden, like Lucy or Mina in Stoker's *Dracula*, similarly drawn into the sexual perversity of her pursuer as the woman chosen by the vampire is drawn to his need for her blood. The only reason Millhone is able to escape is that Messinger appears to savor this game of terror foreplay without climax, and elects on this particular occasion not to kill her.

But Millhone is forced into intimate physical contact with him once more at the end of the novel. Millhone notes that Messinger holds her in the same way as her protector Dietz has done, suggesting the attraction and repulsion of the Double as lover/destroyer (322). When Messinger grips her, "I could smell the tawny sweat of sex oozing out of his pores" (324). Messinger abducts Millhone as a pawn in his search for his son. She is eventually rescued, not by her lover Dietz, but by another woman: Mark's wife, Rochelle Messinger.

What Millhone acknowledges in her ambivalent response to Messinger is her fascination with the creatures at the bottom of the criminal investigation. Like Poe, she explores the depths: "Beware the dark pool at the bottom of our hearts. In its icy, black depths dwell strange and twisted creatures it is best not to disturb. With this investigation, I was once again uncomfortably aware that in probing into murky waters I was exposing myself to the predators lurking therein" (*"I" Is for Innocent* 177). Like a heroine from one of Ann Radcliffe's novels, she has the capacity for terrifying herself with a Gothic imagination: a "bloodied hand reaching through [a broken window] to turn the latch" (*"G" I for Gumshoe* 128), and she appreciates the power of fear's contagion: "a phenomenon magnified by proximity, which is why horror movies are so potent in a crowded theater" (*"G"* 241). Her images of fear come right out of Poe: "I was beginning to feel about the real world as I did about swimming in the ocean.

Off the Santa Teresa coast, the waters of the Pacific are murky and cold, filled with USTs (unidentified scary things) that can hurt you real bad: organisms made of jelly and slime, crust-covered creatures with stingers and horny pincers that can rip your throat out. Mark Messinger was like that: vicious, implacable, dead at heart" (*"G"* 177).

The female detective's quest, then, is to overcome that secret sea creature lurking in her heart, and in so doing, to break free of the restrictive gender oppression of the Gothic heroine. The way to this liberation is found in solving the mystery; Gothic villains and criminals must be punished or exposed in some appropriate way for the detective to resume control over her own life and for peace to be restored to her world.

The haunted interior chambers of Poe's horror tales have been recast into the mean streets of the detective tale. While the style of building may have altered, the biology of place remains consistently central to the tales. While women detective writers do not travel these mean streets as often as the hard-boiled male detectives, they are still acquainted with them, as when Warshawski goes into the Lion's Den in *Bitter Medicine*. There she is subject to the victimization by Sergio discussed above. Paretsky's version of the Poe mansion is the ironically named Friendship hospital. Its evil core is guarded by starched repellent nurses whose main job is to protect the doctors from outside intruders. The nurses use the institutional bureaucracy—the sea of forms that must be filled out to the point of numbness—to preclude access to the workings of the hospital's central administration. Warshawski brings Consuelo Alvarez to Friendship because of a medical emergency and gets her treatment, but it is inadequate and Alvarez and her baby die. Later, Warshawski breaks into the hospital at night, steals into Burgoyne's office, and finds the information she needs, but to garner these data she must break into the institution's protective system of exclusion by posing as a white-coated doctor. She must resort to stealing records from Humphries' and Burgoyne's offices and, assuming the role of a secretary, copies them on the machine (a male detective would simply have lifted the records and gone off with them). To gain access into the hospital, Warshawski must take on a traditional female role: posing as a secretary to operate the copying machine and then to gain information about who is paying some legal bills. The hospital itself, looming like some imposing haunted mansion overlooking its expansive parking lot, is filled with rooms, offices, places off limits (Vic avoids a restricted zone in order to avoid infecting the patients), and is dominated by the novel's version of the Gothic monster/villain personified in Alan Humphries.

Millhone encounters a more traditional haunted house in *"G" Is for Gumshoe*: the Bronfen House. The place itself has a history of murder and secrets contained within. It has a potting shed with the remains of a corpse buried in its dark moistness. The house itself is inhabited by old men who board here, shuffling their way through the ends of their lives like ghosts.

The structure is filled with furniture from the last century; once-white curtains hung in "limp wisps." And under the kitchen wallpaper which Millhone strips away are drab rivulets of rust-colored blood from an old murder. These are details more typical of the horror tale than the detective. They are, however, certainly reminiscent of Poe's haunted chambers filled with ghostly-animated knights in shining armor and grotesque tapestries that appear to possess a life of their own, as in "Ligeia," or the evidence of murder and interment of the already decaying body in "The Black Cat."

Poe's tales subvert traditional patriarchal authority by undermining the conventions of marriage ("The Black Cat") or the relations between master and servant ("The Tell-Tale Heart"). The hysteria built by the pressure of those institutional constructs was enough to break through the walls of reason to overcome the narrators. Montressor lives his fifty years without his murder being discovered because he can use the very institutions whose representative, Fortunato, he has destroyed. And the café detective of "The Man of the Crowd" sums up the institutional patriarchy by seeing clerks, gamblers, respectable men and others hurrying through the streets as he observes and classifies them. But, even as he questions these institutions, Poe leaves the reader, having experienced vicariously the thrill of destruction, to adopt them once more: The murderous narrators of "The Black Cat" and "The Tell-Tale Heart" are in custody and will have their punishments.

Paretsky directly attacks patriarchal institutions in each of her novels. The institutions she depicts are inherently corrupt—as is the case with the for-profit Friendship hospital in *Bitter Medicine*—torn between providing health care for sick patients and money for its stockholders at the same time. In her canon, the author questions the integrity of the insurance industry, the shipping business on the Great Lakes, the Church, the chemical industry, even the system of tunnels that provides protection against floods for the city of Chicago. And she subverts all these corporate organizations not only by questioning their integrity, but working from within the institutions themselves to bring them down. The villains in her narratives are those individuals, mostly men such as Peter Burgoyne, who have pledged their souls to these companies in return for power and financial largesse. Peter Burgoyne appears to be respectable, but he has been corrupted by the soft seduction of money. Alan Humphries, his colleague, is perhaps even more corrupt because he is closer to the power center of the hospital. Again, he appears as normal as the politically corrupt Tom Coulter, whose old-boy network keeps Friendship Hospital in business. These villains emerge from the bureaucratic system, the hospital, and their commitment to maintaining the secrets and corruption of the system emerges out of a perverse combination of institutional loyalty and self-preservation.

In place of the usual social construct of marriage and family, women detective writers impose a web of social inter-relationships. The detective story often involves a sense of loss and, in the final reestablishment of order, of something regained. Grafton's Millhone is twice divorced and grows ever-more suspicious of the family she has left but that refuses to leave her in the ongoing alphabet of crime series; Paretsky's Warshawski has been divorced from Dick Yarborough, who returns occasionally but is not part of Vic's network. Both detectives have an older male protector. Mr. Contreros, Warshawski's downstairs neighbor, keeps watch over her without the potential intrusion of a sexual relationship that a younger man might come to represent. Millhone's landlord, Henry Pitts, bakes bread and provides a companionship, again without entanglements. Both women have occasional lovers, close friends (Lotty Herschel for Vic, Vera for Kinsey), and other associates to provide them with assistance, networking, and the comforts we associate with personal lives. Against the disintegration of family and social world that characterize many Gothic tales, these substitute families provide a measure of integration, love, and support.

One of the functions of this networking is to counter Poe's sense of isolation. The reason these women detectives do not succumb to Gothic terror is because of their networking. Their solid social structure confirms them within the world. It helps them to obtain information that is converted and used as a weapon in the women's tales. Warshawski gets her confession through displaying Burgoyne's notes on a screen at a medical conference. Millhone finds a clue on a microfilm reader in the library. She also understands more because the names of the Brontë sisters are used as a kind of code. The reliance upon male violence is never an ultimate solution for women detectives. Even Warshawski's final shootout at Humphries' office is dominated, not by the woman detective, but by the male policeman, Rawlings.

Detective fiction has had a history of moving from an adversarial relationship with the police to one of cooperation and even to the induction of the detective to the police force itself. Dupin heaps scorn on the police in "The Murders in the Rue Morgue," but he cooperates with them in "The Purloined Letter." Sherlock Holmes maintains a distinct rivalry with the authorities, while the male hard-boiled school has established an uneasy working relationship with the police. Women detectives tend to depend on the police, or other men, more partly because of their smaller physical stature and their antipathy to the level of violence that marks the hard-boiled style. The hard-boiled males remain loners; the hard-boiled females look to establish colleagues as well as friends.

As is the case with the evolution of the detective tale, the contemporary horror story is often distinguished from that of earlier generations in its representations of women. Since its inception, the Gothic story has evoked its thrills at the expense of women; traditionally, the Gothic heroine was the (present or future) wife of the hero. Her particular terror stimulated the Gothic villain's imagination as well as his libido and inspired the hero to a suitably heroic rescue. Thus, Isabella's fate and chastity are preserved in Walpole's *Castle of Otranto* through the intercession of Theodore; Mina Harker's virtues as both wife and Victorian woman are restored in Stoker's *Dracula* through the efforts of her husband and his male colleagues.

The contemporary Gothic female, similar to what we have traced in considering the distinctive role of the female detective, often finds herself out on her own; she must confront the monster without the aid of a heroic male. In her discussion of gender dynamics in contemporary horror films, Carol Clover describes this shift toward independent resolve in the new Gothic heroine. Her observations about the "Final Girl" in slasher films apply elsewhere in contemporary horror art:

> By 1980, the male rescuer is either dismissably marginalized or dispensed with altogether; not a few films have him rush to the rescue only to be hacked to bits, leaving the Final Girl to save herself after all. At the moment that the Final Girl becomes her own savior, she becomes a hero; . . . Abject terror may still be gendered feminine, but the willingness of one immensely popular current genre to re-represent the hero as an anatomical female would seem to suggest that at least one of the traditional marks of heroism, triumphant self-rescue, is no longer strictly gendered masculine. (60)

In contemporary Gothic novels such as Stephen King's *Gerald's Game*, *Dolores Claiborne*, and *Rose Madder*; Christopher Fowler's "The Master Builder"; Thomas Harris's *The Silence of the Lambs*; and films such as *Alien, Halloween*, and *Kiss the Girls*, the female protagonist's courage and wits are severely tested. They remain her primary weapons against the intrusive force of the male monster. Her survival is tied directly to how well she employs them.

While each of the texts listed above features strong and independent women characters who break from traditional Gothic gender stereotypes, the authors/directors of these texts are nevertheless all men. Contemporary women writers of horror fiction have produced a corpus of work that is at least as interesting and diverse as women detective authors. Surely the contributions of Anne Rice, Kathie Koja, and Poppy Z. Brite alone have provided new self-fashioned characters, thematic orientations, and reconfigurations of horror tropes that have broadened the possibilities of the Gothic, expanding the genre beyond its traditional male biases. Anne

Rice's fictional creatures have entered the *zeitgeist* of the twentieth century and continue on into the third millennium—as vampires, witches, mummies, and ghouls who are at the same time unique story tellers, philosophers, cultural critics, and struggling personalities (Haas 66). But for the purposes of this book, Rice, Koja, and Brite, while deeply reliant upon the Gothic, would appear to share only the most obvious of connections to Edgar Poe: phantasmagorical settings, a fascination with evoking various forms of terror in the reader, and an obsessional preoccupation with the dying and the undead. The closest female descendant of Poe writing today is Joyce Carol Oates, who acknowledges her debt to Poe not only in the quotation that fronts this chapter but throughout her prolific canon of literary essays, poems, short fiction, and novels. Indeed, Oates frequently superimposes Poe's plotlines consciously upon her own material.

Oates is close to Poe in her capacity and propensity for evoking states of psychological turmoil and assaults upon character identity. The *Atlantic* magazine has called Oates "the dark lady of American letters" (Ballamy 63), and in terms of the violence alone that threatens to overcome so many of her tales, she is both an archetypically American author and a dark chronicler of the various fractures that are currently splitting her society. "I wish the world were a prettier place," Oates has remarked, "but I wouldn't be honest as a writer if I ignored the actual conditions around me" (Graham 406). Her protagonists often find themselves at points of deep spiritual trauma that give birth to radical self-consciousness. "Crazy" is a favorite word in her novels and short narratives, and many of her characters live just on the boundaries of sanity as they struggle to establish a sense of control over their lives. Like Poe, she probes the dark side of human nature, the mysterious depths of the unconscious, and the primitive brutality at the core of physical existence (Creighton xi).

Oates has created a group of characters who are haunted—essentially preoccupied with something that frequently pushes them all to the point of distraction or into the realm of obsession. So many of her protagonists are drawn into the realm of the perverse: men who obsess and stalk, women who must confront their most repressed urges, the unresolved anxieties of frightening childhoods and nightmarish marriages. In Poe, such intimate levels of psychic wounding give birth to crime or psychosis. This sometimes occurs in Oates's fiction as well, although in many tales her protagonists are forced simply to endure the unsettling situations that border the perimeters of terror.

Dr. Larry Prior in the tale "Bloodstains" holds much in common with Poe's narrators who suffer psychological distress. While Prior never deliberately conspires to commit a homicide, he suffers from a Poe-like sense of self-fragmentation and loss of mental stability. The tale's cryptic allusions to his wife's possible infidelity (although this remains unproven) slowly erode his self-confidence; as a consequence, his patients' maladies come to mirror his own personal disintegration. As one of them remarks, echoing Prior's own encroaching philosophy: "'There isn't any point. I don't see it. We are all running out, people our age, things are running out of us . . . draining out of us . . . I will have to live out my life in this body'" (177).

"Bloodstains" takes its title from Dr. Prior's discovery of a pair of his daughter's underwear stained with the blood of her menstrual cycle: "Then it occurs to him that his daughter was ashamed to put these soiled underpants in the wash, that she had meant to wash them herself but had forgotten" (179). The underwear poses an unsettling mystery for this father, who, like many of Oates's parents, is completely estranged from the inner life of his daughter. His gendered isolation from offspring and wife again recalls so many of Poe's male narrators who are made to feel emotionally isolated from the women in their lives.

Similarly, in the story "The Dungeon," we are introduced to an artist figure who, like many of the masculine voices found in Poe's poetry and narratives, and perhaps most like Poe himself, is an angry isolato who feels trapped in a world of bourgeois conventions and values. "The Dungeon," it turns out, is a self-imposed place: the realm of the artist's hypersensitive mind. In any event, the tale forms a contemporary link to a literary line that begins with Poe's aggressively self-tormented narrators, and goes on to include Dostoevsky's underground men, Baudelaire's apocalyptic urbanites, and Kafka's alienated hunger artists.

Oates's narrator struggles to connect with a woman named Eleanor, who appears to share many of the same restorative capacities found in Poe's poem, "Eleanora." Written through a series of interiorized mental fragments that force the reader into the subjective realm of Oates's protagonist, the latter struggles to reveal through his diary entries the condition of his tortured soul to Eleanor. His desire to communicate with her, however, is always fraught with a tension that borders on Gothic violence: "Embarrassed little Eleanor one of the safe soulless tidy ones, little bitch, aren't you Eleanor, are you reading this far Eleanor, so prudently withdrawing your 'friendship' from me as if I DID NOT EXIST any longer. One minute we are friends (& you hoped perhaps for an engagement ring, I suppose—to show your envious pop-eyed friends), the next minute we are ex-friends" (146). The narrator's aggressive literary posture toward Eleanor (and the larger world) is highly ambivalent throughout. It indicates both a cry for sympathy and companionship (why else insist that she read his ravings?) that echoes back to those various desperate attempts in Poe where the quest to form intimate bonds with women (and reader alike) are deliberately undermined by virtue of the artist's fierce egotism and self-destructive compulsions.

Oates continually underscores the obsessional gender antipathy that is central to so many of Poe's tales of terror. It is possible to trace through Oates's work a career-long obsession with rape, incest, and sexual violence against women—analogs to central issues found throughout Poe's fiction. In perhaps her best-known story, "Where are You Going, Where Have You Been?", Connie resembles closely a contemporary version of the classic Gothic heroine. Like one of Mrs. Radcliffe's fanciful young females, Connie possesses an active imagination that delights in the innocent thrill of romantic encounters: "Connie sat with her eyes closed in the sun, dreaming and dazed with the warmth about her as if this were a kind of love, the caresses of love, and her mind slipped into thoughts of the boy she had been with the night before and how nice he had been" (122).

Connie encounters the story's requisite Gothic villain, Arnold Friend, when he comes to her home to complete a seduction that began when he first observed her several days earlier walking out of a restaurant. His arrival interrupts her daydream; in fact, he appears to emerge from it. As is often the role of the Gothic villain/monster, Friend represents the subconsciously erotic shadow of the horror maiden's puerile fantasies and play-acting. He is the Gothic Ravager—the monstrous male libido—a close kin to Poe's compulsive narrator in "Berenice," whose obsession with female molars crosses over into psychotic fetish worship and murder. Representing the long line of Gothic males who precede him, from Lewis's Ambrosio to Stoker's Dracula, the hypnotic Friend does not seek friendship from Connie; he wants nothing less than her complete capitulation. Her foreshadowed rape and murder at his hands will make this possession complete. And like Dracula and Satan himself, Friend requires Connie to enter his world by surrendering her own volition. His design of domination appears to require her own collusion: "'I ain't made plans for coming in that house where I don't belong but just for you to come out to me, the way you should. Don't you know who I am?'" (132). Perhaps the true terror of this tale is not in the nightmarish projection of Connie's sexual fantasies, but that in her violation Friend seeks to despoil her sexual innocence at the same time as he violates her very personhood.

As the first half of this chapter illustrates, in the contemporary detective novel women detectives have become Gothic rescuers. Critic Michelle A. Masse argues that the situation of the traditional Gothic heroine has been reinvigorated by the initiative and activity of the contemporary feminist detective, the latter "insisting on bringing once invisible, 'domestic,' oppression to justice as the social crime it is" (273). Increasingly over the years, Oates's fiction has endeavored to redress the "domestic oppression" that frequently characterizes growing up female in America.

In a collection of short stories, *Haunted: Tales of the Grotesque*, for example, Oates indites the consumer fetishism of male culture that turns women into commodity products enslaved by constricting images of beauty and encouraged to participate in their own submission. Oates poses several female characters in the position where they not only struggle against their male oppressors, but do so with a premeditated violence that even exceeds what these women themselves have experienced at the hands of fathers, boyfriends, and husbands. These are tales organized around the theme of feminized terror, where women are monsters as well as victims. As she remarks in the volume's "Afterword: Reflections on the Grotesque": evil "has the power to make us not simply victims, as nature and accidents do, but active accomplices" (306).

"The Premonition," one of the best stories in *Haunted*, is as much a tale of revenge and violence as anything found in Poe. It is essentially a feminized version of "The Cask of Amontillado," "The Tell-Tale Heart," or "Hop-Frog," wherein a wife and her daughters finally obtain their freedom from a tyrant husband/father who has physically abused and psychologically manipulated their lives for years.

The story also owes something to the detective genre as well as it has a Watson-like narrator through whom the narrative is filtered, observed, interpreted, and biased. This character, Whitney Paxton, has a dark premonition one December night because of rumors that his brother, Quinn, is drinking excessively and threatening the safety of Ellen, his wife, and their two daughters. The narrative details plenty of reasons for Whitney's nervousness: his brother's temper, possessiveness, alcoholism, and propensity for violence. But Whitney's naivete is as much a part of this story as is his brother's boorish behavior. It never occurs to him that Ellen, as a female, is capable of protecting herself, or that his horrible premonition may indeed be solidly grounded—he has just misinterpreted the roles of victim and victimizer.

Early on we learn that Ellen epitomizes the affluent, sophisticated American female: "Ellen was unfailingly glamorous—a quiet, reserved, beautiful woman who took obsessive care with grooming and clothes, and whose very speech patterns seemed premeditated. Quinn liked women in high heels—good-looking women, at least—so Ellen rarely appeared in anything other than stylishly high heels, even at casual gatherings" (178). This information is significant for several reasons. First, it shows us that Ellen has worked hard at trying to please her husband. But her willingness to do so by wearing high heels implies a certain level of submissive vulnerability that is often associated with being fashionably feminine in American culture. Thus, her appearance is made to contrast sharply with the aggressive action she eventually takes against her husband, and this discrepancy is a major reason for Whitney's inability to interpret events correctly. She falls out of the role Whitney attributes to her, that of long-suffering abuse victim, to take her fate into her own hands. As Barbara Soukup argues, such a "stark violation of the habitual power distribution in her marriage is totally inconceivable to Whitney—so much so that he fails to recognize it when he arrives at the scene" (11). Ellen's submissive vulnerability clearly extends only to her choice of footwear; her stiletto heels are not a completely accurate signifier of her personality. Cast in this context, it is of some significance that on the night Whitney visits the Paxton home Ellen surprises him by wearing "flat-heeled shoes," a subtle symbol of her marital and gender rebellion (178).

Throughout the tale, Oates raises several disquieting gender stereotypes, only to undermine them systematically. Whitney is a well-intentioned and empathetic brother-in-law and bachelor uncle (he himself has suffered severely under Quinn's tyranny), but he does not have many "wits" when it comes to understanding women. He keeps referring to females in broad generalizations—"How characteristic of women, how sweet, that they trust as they do" (187)—that indicate his bachelorhood has precluded important insights into the nature of women. Nor is he a very good detective, as he fails miserably in piecing together the same evidence that leads the reader to conclude that Quinn has been murdered and dismembered by the female members of his own family: the garden and barbeque tools found in the kitchen in December, the omnipresent smell of blood, the near hysteria of the women themselves, that both Ellen and her daughters bear bruises on their faces, and that the family has also found out about Quinn's adulterous betrayal: Trish's miscue about the "Sea Shell Islands" (182) confirms that the women are already aware of what Whitney has heard as a rumor. Through Whitney's dimwitted observations, Oates challenges the gender assumptions that individual women are incapable of joining forces against patriarchal authority; that because of their physical stature, the only recourse against an abusive husband/father is to put up with his abuse or leave him, rather than answer his behavior in kind; and, perhaps most upsetting, particularly for her male readership, that these "three attractive, sweet-faced women" are not the simple "benign Fates" that Whitney (and most men) trust women to be (185).

The story takes place in the kitchen of the Paxton mansion during the Christmas season. These background facts are extremely important as they further serve to undercut Whitney's stereotypical views on women. The kitchen, aside from being the center of any home, is traditionally associated with female domesticity; Christmas, the season of peace and love, also often revolves around a wife and mother's attentiveness in preparing the festive meals and decorating presents in the home. In "The Premonition," both the kitchen and Christmas are recast into grotesque parodies of delicate feminine servitude. All of the expensively-wrapped Christmas presents Ellen and her daughters are assembling bear selected parts of the man they have recently dismembered in the kitchen. These women are sending their husband and father, piece by piece, back to his family, those individuals who were largely responsible for creating the adult monster that Quinn Paxton became and then who did nothing to curb his scurrilous behavior. (The reader can only speculate gleefully what part of Quinn ended up in Whitney's box.) Ellen appears to have taught her daughters a new family Yuletide recipe, passing down a heaping helping of revenge from one generation of females to another.

As a tale of revenge, Oates's story owes much to the ironic subtexts that characterize Poe's "The Cask of Amontillado" and "The Tell-Tale Heart." Like Montressor in "Amontillado," whose conversational skills are amusingly ironic throughout the descent into the family wine vault, Ellen Paxton possesses a dark sense of humor to go along with her capacity for violent retribution. The special packages Ellen and her daughters assemble for their Paxton relatives to open under their trees on Christmas morning (one would imagine with an "Open Me First" label attached) are prepared with a distinctly Poe-esque appreciation for the macabre. That this is a tale specifically about a woman's revenge also suggests a certain parallel to "The Tell-Tale Heart," if we accept the distinct possibility that Poe's narrator in this story is female rather than male. Poe critics have generally regarded the narrator as male, but since the sex of the speaker is indeterminate, there is no reason why the narrator could not be a woman, as scholar Gita Rajan was first to speculate, whose whole life has been a confinement in a dark house under the officious and accusing vulture-like eye of a patriarchal figure (283–300). If this is indeed the situation, it provides a strong feminist context for explaining the level of emancipation that Ellen Paxton, her daughters, and Poe's narrator share in common after they commit their respective homicides.

Oates shares Poe's awareness of love's underside, of its longing and loss. In both her fiction and poetry, love is frequently a violent and destructive energy. As Poe's poems and tales often speak of unfulfilled and therefore unsatisfying unions between men and women, Oates writes of love similarly, of the tragic link between love and self-obliteration. In Poe's love poems and amorous narratives, men obsess about women dead, dying, or prematurely buried. Their condition is a hellish experience, but one that also brings Poe's romantic males a certain headiness of delusion: their lives take on meaning only in the immortal image of a lost Lenore or Annabelle Lee, the urge to be supernaturally reunited with the Lady Ligeia, or the acute awareness of a dead sister's imminent resurrection from the grave. Many of Oates's tales, as well as her poems, share this sensibility, but in her work these masculine obsessions transcend the essentially passive ghost worship we find in Poe to a more active and prosaic response: anger, possessive jealousy, and violence. As the writer herself has speculated: "Bad as it is to fall hopelessly in love with someone unattainable, it is far worse to be the innocent object of someone's (unattainable) love. Then you feel yourself hunted, boxed-up, continually *thought about;* you realize that you are part of someone's fantasy, uncontrollable by himself or by you, and this is truly terrifying" (Milazzo 58).

In Poe's "The Black Cat," the marital conflict between the male narrator and his wife is gradually sublimated into antagonism against the cat, not only a favorite pet of his wife's, but, more importantly a symbol of the feminine that the narrator grows to detest. As a result, all of the narrator's insecurities as a male and as a husband find expression in his antipathy toward the cat. The fact that we only learn about the existence of his spouse when she tries to protect the cat suggests the level of their marital intimacy.

In Oates's story "The White Cat," the thematic and gender intertextual correspondences with Poe's tale are readily presented. Like Poe's narrator, Oates's Julian Muir harbors ambivalent feelings toward his much younger, beautiful, and gregarious spouse, Alissa. From the beginning of the tale it is clear that Muir associates the cat's affection toward others, particularly male friends of his wife, with Alissa's own growing emotional indifference toward him and natural attraction to other men: "He'd thought that husband and wife were one flesh in more than merely the metaphorical sense of that term. Yet it happened that his own marriage was a marriage of a decidedly diminished sort. Marital relations had all but ceased, and there seemed little likelihood of their being resumed" (82). Like Poe's insecure and tempestuous husband in "The Black Cat," Muir's anger toward the cat, Miranda, is a sublimated extension of his violent, albeit repressed, urges against his wife. Both husbands view marital loyalty in terms of jealous ownership: their wives, like their cats, belong to a patriarchal order and are therefore mere chattel whose fates are to be determined according to a male design: "One day, watching her rubbing about the ankles of a director-friend of his wife's, observing how wantonly she presented herself to an admiring little circle of guests, Mr. Muir found himself thinking that, as he had brought the cat into the household of his own volition and paid a fair amount of money for her, she was his to dispose of as he wished" (74).

Miranda's "wanton" behavior with Alissa's guests feeds Muir's suspicions about his wife—the sexual implications of Miranda's feline friendliness is meant to underscore Muir's insecurities about his marriage and Alissa's sexual fidelity. His consequent obsession with killing the cat neatly parallels the homicidal motivations Poe's narrator expresses in "The Black

Cat": both men seek to destroy that which they cannot control—specifically, the feminine principle. Their respective wives represent those characteristics in themselves that each husband has systematically repressed: sensitivity, a concern and respect for others, artistic expression, an appreciation of the beautiful, the need for social connections. Content to live their lives in isolation, these men are not merely possessively jealous over their wives, they also recognize them as independent agents that threaten the male microcosms these men have created.

These tales of cats are really two tales of men who demand desperately to be at the center of a universe of their own making. Poe's narrator wallows in gin to fashion a world of dark indulgence. Muir uses his money and its control over an impressionable young actress to make himself into a godhead. The problem for both these men is that their wives simply refuse to go along with their plans; the women are, like the cats they resemble and admire, neither predictable nor easily dominated. In fact, both Oates and Poe appear to imply in each cat tale that a man's love for a woman is closely aligned to a human's relationship with a cat: the harder a human seeks to force his will upon a cat, the less likely he is to inspire feline affection and loyalty: "But of course, as Alissa acknowledged, a cat can't be forced to do anything against her will. 'It seems almost to be a law of nature,' she said solemnly" (83). Perhaps this helps explain why both men ultimately fail to destroy their respective pets and end up in worse circumstances than where they began (Poe's narrator in jail for murder, Muir a victim of a botched suicide now confined to a wheelchair). The cats and wives in both these tales represent feminine principles, perhaps akin to life itself, that when either thwarted or violently repressed only leads to male self-destruction.

As much as Poe writes fiction about and from the perspective of a masculine-centered universe, Joyce Carol Oates writes stories about the lives of women, particularly their fears and conflicts. Some of these anxieties are universal—i.e., shared with men—but what is most important about her work is Oates's ability to capture those specific terrors that belong to middle-class, white, affluent, and educated females who would seem to be safely insulated from such assaults. In her novels and stories, the Gothic is confronted by contemporary women whose lives are, at least on the surface, anything but horrific. But as with Poe and Emily Dickinson, to whom she is often compared, the horror aesthetic in Oates is an interior condition, a terror of the soul, rather than an exterior, or supernatural imposition. Oates possesses tremendous insight into the shadowed regions of the human psyche; she illuminates the dark realities of modern life as experienced from the perspective of being female. While many of her tales are shaped by a feminist sensibility that insists that to be a daughter or a wife means something quite different from being a son or husband, she is also acutely aware that women are no more immune than men from violent impulses or perverse behavior.

The Gothic permeates her fictional world. Her female protagonists are perhaps better equipped to struggle against patriarchal oppression than were women from earlier Gothic romances, but the fact remains that they are still struggling with many of the same issues: repressed urges, masculine possessiveness and violence, the cycle of self-destructive motivation. A liberal feminist might argue that these issues remain yet unresolved because American culture still reflects the restrictive limits of masculine authority. But both female Gothic and detective writers are exploring the soft edges of social relationships, pushing a feminine sensibility into an essentially masculine tradition. Human nature may be unchangeable, but exploring a feminist orientation allows for a deeper appreciation of possibilities. While feminist Gothic and detective genres may not pose ultimate solutions to a static human nature, they are at least capable of shedding new light from out of the shadows.

Chapter 5

Proportioning Poe:
The Blurring of Horror and Detection in
The Silence of the Lambs

Gore is everywhere. And with the widespread dissemination of gore the body remains the central marker upon which we articulate the spectacular degradation of everyday life. (Crane 159–60)

The terror of gender is carried even further by Thomas Harris in *The Silence of the Lambs* (1988). Not only is the detective, Clarice Starling, a woman pursued by serial killer Buffalo Bill (a.k.a. Jame Gumb), she is also caught between two male teachers each of whom wants to use her and dominate her. Starling lives within a patriarchal world, controlled by men whose standards she has to meet. As an FBI trainee, she has to keep up with her course work with the threat of being "recycled" constantly looming over her. As an admirer of Jack Crawford, she carries the extra burden of interviewing Hannibal Lecter. When she lets Lecter into her head, she responds, first to his *quid pro quo* game, then to his clues to capture Buffalo Bill.

From the beginning of the novel, we are made aware of Clarice as a woman operating in a male domain. On her way to visit Lecter in prison, she is verbally assaulted by the male prisoners and by Dr. Chilton's patronizing commentary. She avoids Chilton's awkward attempt to set up another, possible romantic meeting even when her compliance could serve her purposes. Her spirit of independence is apparent from the outset and is maintained in spite of her own self-criticism: "*He might know something useful. It wouldn't have hurt her to simper once, even if she wasn't good at it*" (9). As she approaches Lecter's cell, she is painfully aware of herself as outsider-female, "knowing her heels announced her" (14). Once she is in front of him, Lecter proceeds to examine intimate facets of her person—from her choice of perfume to the quality of her handbag and shoes.

Why does Harris underscore so much gender consciousness so early in the novel? Most obviously, because this is a book that centers around women, particularly those gender traits that distinguish women from men. And if Starling hopes to capture the man who preys on women, she must somehow transform the daily anger and outrage she feels as a woman into something useful: "All of Buffalo Bill's victims were women, his obsession was women, he lived to hunt women. Not one woman was hunting him full time. Not one woman investigator had looked at every one of his crimes. Starling wondered if Crawford would have the nerve to use her as a technician when he had to go look at Catherine Martin. Bill would 'do her tomorrow,' Crawford predicted. *Do her. Do her. Do her.* 'Fuck this,' Starling said aloud and put her feet on the floor" (292). This moment in the book is important as it reveals Clarice's motivation and determination to become an active agent in Buffalo Bill's capture rather than return to her role as a passive female student at the FBI academy. At this point in the narrative, she is officially off the case, back at school. But her raised gender consciousness, that commenced with pity and sympathy for Buffalo Bill's victims and slowly metamorphosed into a personalized identification with them as women as much as victims, motivates Starling to stay on the case. In a novel about transformation and gender identification, Starling is as much affected by her association with his victims as is Buffalo Bill himself.

Any discussion of *The Silence of the Lambs* must include at least mention of the negative criticism that has surrounded the text, especially in light of the film adaptation that swept the 1992 Academy Awards. A post-Academy Award editorial in *The Nation* condemned the film as an amoral, politically incorrect movie that "trumpets sadomasochism, homophobia, misogyny, and worse" (507). The narrative's graphic level of violence perpetuated against women was the subject of detective novelist Sara Paretsky's article written for the op-ed section of the *New York Times*. She expressed her dissatisfaction with both Harris's work and those women readers who purchased it: "So, why should I be surprised that women are paying to read about a man flaying women alive and stripping off their skins? That's what we're doing. And we're doing it enough to make *The Silence of the Lambs* a best seller. . . . Why do women as well as men want to read about these exploits in vivid detail that seeks to recreate the pain and humiliation of the attack?" (17).

Silence does portray homosexuality in an exclusively negative light; since the narrative contains no healthy homosexual experiences or characterizations, homoeroticism is linked inextricably to pathology. On a more positive note, however, *The Silence of the Lambs* is much more than just another tale of misogynistic horror and violent titillation, and to so limit it does both book and film a grave disservice. In fact, in the end these texts have more in common with the heroic quest—to create a world of greater security and beauty where women need not be afraid—than they do with the recreation of pain and humiliation. Paretsky seemingly ignores the major contribution Clarice Starling makes to *Silence*, thereby overlooking a potential answer to her own rhetorical questions: women readers are drawn to Harris's novel because they strongly identify with Starling.

Starling is "toughened" by her contact with men. As a result, she comes to know the men in this book better than they, even the one who wishes to possess a woman suit, ever learn to know women. And, of course, she is angered and frustrated by what she learns. Hannibal Lecter asks her—

"'how do you manage your rage?'"(169)—a question that becomes as important to Clarice as it is to the meddlesome psychiatrist. For Clarice is surrounded by men who either patronize women or murder them: Lecter, Crawford, Buffalo Bill, Chilton, and the male-dominated bureaucracy of the FBI itself. Without a conscious effort to exercise self-control and discipline, contact with these men and their patriarchal institutions might have produced a woman overwhelmed by her rage against male sexism and aggression.

But this is not what happens. Harris's book is not only about the screaming of lambs; it is also about their silencing. Starling must somehow silence the rage she feels toward men. The silence she finds does not come from repression, sublimation, or contribution to the madness by becoming a crazed anti-male avenger who seeks to punish all men for the random carnage of a few. Instead, Starling assumes control over her anger by pursuing what she can change, in herself as well as in the world. As we will soon document, Starling learns a great deal from both her teachers, Hannibal Lecter and Jack Crawford. And certainly their degrees of mutual self-confidence and focused intensity become models for Starling. By so centering her energies and emotions, she comes to interpret Buffalo Bill as a symbol for the perversity that men perpetuate upon women, behavior that Starling understands intimately and translates into an empathetic bond with Buffalo Bill's female victims.

Detective-trainee Clarice Starling begins in the patriarchal world of the FBI, dependent. She is a student selected to carry out the questioning of Hannibal Lecter. Crawford selects her partly because of their association in a seminar in which Starling was enrolled at the University of Virginia. He also selects her because, as Dr. Chilton points out, Lecter hasn't seen a woman in years. Crawford can use Starling for his own psychiatric ends, gaining either information from Lecter about himself or about Buffalo Bill. Both Lecter and Crawford represent two competing parts of the same figure. While the two men appear to manipulate Starling as a vehicle in their continuing mental warfare against each other, thereby deepening the novel's theme of women being exploited by men, they also occupy remarkably similar roles insofar as they emerge as competing father figures and teachers to Starling. In "The Purloined Letter" Poe emphasizes the identification of detective and criminal; the way Dupin locates the letter is by thinking in the same way that Minister D_____ does. The identification of these two men leads to their being like two sides of the same coin: for Poe the difference was political; for Harris, the difference is moral, between good and evil. Crawford competes with Lecter, using Starling to get as much information as possible about Buffalo Bill. Lecter, in turn, uses Crawford as a roundabout way of effecting his escape. Both work through Starling, and each is jealous of the other. Crawford's last appearance in the novel has him warning Starling to protect herself from Lecter: "'You know he'd do it to you, just like he'd do anybody else'" (356). When Starling says Lecter won't bushwhack her because it would be rude, Crawford does not understand.

Like Sherlock Holmes, Lecter knows many things from his own experience and professional studies. He gives Starling important information without even looking at the case, such as the fact that Buffalo Bill inhabits a two-story house or that he would scalp his victims. But Lecter has a rival: Crawford is competing for Starling. Crawford explains that Lecter was safe in predicting that Bill would take scalps. Because Lecter didn't specify a time, he could never be wrong: "'If we caught Bill and there was no scalping, Lecter could say that we caught him just before he did it.'" Crawford agrees with Lecter that Bill lives in a two-story house because two of the victims were hanged. "'It's very hard for one person to hang another against his will. . . . Tell them you're taking them up to use the bathroom, whatever, walk them up with a hood on, slip the noose on, and boot them off the top step with the rope fastened to the landing railing. It's the only good way in a house'" (93–94).

Crawford instructs the young FBI trainee about detective procedures and, conversely, the importance of knowing when her instincts may be superior to "imposed patterns of symmetry." He informs her, "'Don't let a herd of policemen confuse you. Live right behind your eyes. Listen to yourself'" (76). Like Poe's Dupin, Crawford understands the point at which it is important for the intuitive self to transcend traditional or learned patterns of investigation and thinking. Lecter is likewise interested in teaching Starling valuable information about the criminal psyche, but his approach is always more intrusively intimate, even visceral, and therefore perhaps more impressionable because it strikes to the essence of Starling's personality. Starling needs both her mentors to advance—personally and professionally; through their inimitable pedagogics, they teach her essentially the same thing: the value of balancing self-trust against self-restraint, and the importance of recognizing when to apply either.

Lecter displays jealousy when he asks Starling if Crawford wants her sexually: does he visualize "fucking with you?" Starling says that such a question is of no interest to her (61), but it clearly fascinates Hannibal, and may suggest a certain latent homoerotic attraction that is further underscored in his competition with Crawford for Starling. After all, both men are truly "fucking with" Clarice—metaphorically, if not literally. Lecter's ambivalence toward Crawford is tempered with sympathy; he sends a note to Crawford about his wife Bella, quoting from John Donne's "A Fever" and writing, "I'm so sorry about Bella, Jack" (42). This bond of sympathy and competition is recognized by the two men. Crawford is insightful enough to recognize the danger inherent in allowing Lecter to pass into control of the Tennessee police, but his desire to capture Gumb is desperate enough to risk Lecter's ultimate escape (185). Lecter acknowledges their male bond when he tells Starling, "'you've had Crawford's help and you've had mine'" (61). In spite of their professional competition and mutual involvement with Starling, both men possess an intimate knowledge of one another's professional and personal lives.

Beyond this, Lecter does lead Starling to Jame Gumb. He tells Starling that she has all the materials to catch Buffalo Bill in the file which she hands him. He gives her hints; like the good teacher, he does not spell everything out but encourages the student to draw her own conclusions. He directs her attention to the excessive randomness of the distribution of the bodies. He suggests that this very randomness may hint at a clue to Gumb's thinking. Lecter's implication is that the first murder will lead to where he lives. Starling thus makes a distinction between the first body discovered and the first one taken, Frederica Brimmel. This clue blends in with Lecter's second clue, which he leads up to as he questions Crawford's quotation of Marcus Aurelius. Because Lecter understands the way Gumb's mind works, as Dupin understands the way Minister D____'s mind works, he can direct Starling into talking of first principles. The first principle is that "'we begin by coveting what we see every day'" (226–27). This clue aligns itself in Starling's mind with Lecter's insight into the randomness of corpse distribution, to reveal Buffalo Bill's location.

In turn, Starling gives something back to Lecter: a certain measure of human dignity to an incarcerated man, and this becomes partial explanation for his willingness to aid her. Although the authorities acknowledge the power of his intellect and amoral will, their terror makes it impossible for them to appreciate his humanity; Lecter remains an exotic, albeit dangerous, object to be studied and exploited. While Starling is always willing to exploit him, she also accords him a level of genuine respect that is, ironically, shared elsewhere only by Jame Gumb and another serial killer, Francis Dolarhyde (from the 1981 Harris novel, *Red Dragon*). As critic Greg Garrett argues, "Whether unconsciously or consciously, Clarice, who knows what it's like to be an object, treats Lecter as human rather than object, and the lesson is not lost on him" (8). In their final interview, Starling and Lecter share a moment of intimacy that highlights the balance of respect accorded to each other. When Lecter returns the file to Starling that contains the clues for Gumb's capture, their forefingers touch: "The touch crackled in his eyes. . . . And that is how he remained in Starling's mind. Caught in the instant when he did not mock. Standing in his white cell, arched like a dancer, his hands clasped in front of him and his head slightly to the side" (231).

Poe's contributions to this novel include the inclusion and development of the "police procedural" type of detective story. In "The Purloined Letter," Poe has the Prefect of Police describe the search of Minister D____'s apartment in pursuit of the letter. What the Prefect describes is the procedures of the police, the assiduous search of every possible hiding place—as far as the police understand it. Like the police procedural novels, whose most noted practitioner is Ed McBain and whose methods are followed by such TV programs as *Homicide*, *NYPD Blue*, and *Hill Street Blues*, the method is followed punctiliously. The Minister's apartment is searched over three months: the apartment is searched room by room, the furniture examined minutely, each book in the library is examined page by page. The narrator asks the Prefect details which make him show off his method with pride. Dupin, certain that the method is wrongheaded, humorously advises the Prefect to examine the premises again, which he takes seriously and does.

The police procedural, of which *The Silence of the Lambs* is a partial example, uses its methods because, as Dupin explains, "their own ingenuity is a faithful representative of that of the mass" (218) and therefore solves most of the cases. What Dupin does, as most fictional detectives do who are not part of the police system, is to discover and apply alternative procedures than those employed by the police. This provides the brilliant detective with another angle on the crime that, in turn, puts him on the level of the criminal who is already operating on a different plane from that of the police.

Dupin outwits both criminal and police because of his ability to identify with the criminal imagination; he is, for example, Minister D____'s telluric match and nemesis. This capacity to forge such a psychological identification has become one of the great traditions that the detective genre inherited from Poe. Two decades after Poe's death, the novelist Dostoevsky, who had read Poe and was extremely fond of the latter's detective tales, created in Porfiry Petrovich a Russian version of Dupin, whose true function in *Crime and Punishment* is as a brilliantly sardonic observer of the criminal psyche. Through consistent banter and sarcasm, Porfiry deflates Raskolnikov's pride and extinguishes his illusions. His powers of intellect and insight make him Raskolnikov's equal, if not his superior. Porfiry possesses subtle insight into the murderer and his extraordinary man theories that is unavailable to anyone else in the novel; the repeated jovial interviews that he forces upon Raskolnikov literally wear down the student's spurious resolve and self-control.

From Poe's Dupin, to Dostoevsky's inspector, to Thomas Harris's governmental agents, the gap separating criminal and detective has continued to narrow to the point where the two figures have come to share an intimacy that strikes the reader as both fascinating and disturbing. In

Harris's novel *Red Dragon*, FBI agent Will Graham often appears on the verge of insanity (and has spent some time recovering in an asylum) because of his uncanny ability to identify directly with a criminal pathology. On several occasions, Hannibal Lecter suggests an affinity between himself and the detective, and this parallel so unnerves Graham that he must conscientiously work to repel its implications. Crawford says about Graham that "'Nobody is better with evidence. But he has that other thing too. Imagination, projection, whatever. He doesn't like that part of it'" (8). Relying upon this Dupin-like combination of intelligence and criminal empathy, Graham spends long hours tracing the serial killer's path of destruction, literally forcing himself to re-imagine and re-create the experience that Francis Dolarhyde underwent in the commission of his crimes. By the end of the novel, Graham has established such an unholy connection to Dolarhyde that his mental stability and identity again appear endangered.

True to the detective genre, which has influenced Harris's canon as much as Gothic art, there is a need on the part of his FBI agents to reestablish some palpable order to counterbalance the terror Buffalo Bill, Francis Dolarhyde, and Hannibal Lecter have unleashed upon the world. All of Harris's detectives in *Black Sunday, Red Dragon,* and *The Silence of the Lambs* place themselves in opposition to the destruction and madness that are the consequences of psychopathic behavior. In spite of their unwavering dedication to an essentially moral vision of life, Harris's detectives are nonetheless deeply shaken by their close contact with evil. In the act of solving the crime, his detectives must descend into the darkest regions of their own psyches. Will Graham in *Red Dragon* and Clarice Starling in *Silence* are poised amidst essentially the same struggle: how does one enter the world of madness, identifying with victim and murderer alike, apprehend a killer, and emerge with sanity and humanity intact?

Success in solving their cases parallels the process of detective-criminal identification that we have traced at work from Poe's Dupin to Dostoevsky's Porfiry Petrovich. It is therefore necessary for Starling to "identify fully with the killer, to learn (like any good detective of the genre) to desire what the other desires, to inhabit the place of the other's identifications" (Fuss 93). To accomplish this, Starling must descend within herself, even to the point of blurring identities with Hannibal Lecter. Indeed, through the course of this novel, Lecter becomes a classic detective himself, assisting Starling by providing insights about Gumb, while Starling becomes skilled in the arena of psychopathology.

Starling and Lecter shadow one another, playing mind games against each other for information and the exchange of power. Lecter also leads Starling into intimate psychological contact with Buffalo Bill himself, taking her inside his head and helping her to visualize the design of his madness. Starling learns things from Lecter, but at a potentially terrible price. Crawford warns Starling, "'you tell him no specifics about yourself. You don't want any of your personal facts in his head'" (6). But Lecter does obtain these personal facts, forcing Starling into contact with the negative side of her personality. One of the main elements of the book is Lecter's prying into Starling's past, learning much by observation, more by what Starling tells him. He challenges her to acknowledge her unconscious or repressed self and the unresolved hostility she still harbors toward her childhood: specifically her memory of abandonment and victimization symbolized in her identification with the endangered lambs and the horse, Hannah. This process of confronting the darkness of her childhood ultimately cements a bond with Gumb's victims, who are reminiscent of Starling's innocent lambs led to slaughter for their pelts.

As a woman, Starling identifies with the victims: she discovers clues which no man would think of because of her gender. She identifies with Catherine Martin, whose intimate photos she discovers hidden in a place no man would look: an envelope taped to the underside of the secret drawer in a jewelry box (213). In West Virginia, Starling thinks both like a woman as well as a detective, reasoning, like Sherlock Holmes, from particular details to conclusions: "'Well, she's not a local—her ears are pierced three times each, and she wore glitter polish. Looks like town to me. She's got maybe two weeks or so hair growth on her legs. And see how soft it's grown in? I think she got her legs waxed. Armpits too. Look how she bleached the fuzz on her upper lip'" (84).

Starling willingly follows Lecter into an exploration of her own victimization, past and present, in order to find out who she is: like Dupin identifying himself with the Minister D_____ in order to find out how he thinks, she identifies with Gumb's victims to realize the details of her own life. She identifies with Catherine Martin, both of them being big women (Lecter describes Starling as having "some length of bone" [22]) who would be proper selections for Gumb to choose to make his woman suit. Starling not only stands up for her gender, but uses her gender as empowerment. In West Virginia, she assumes the familiar role of a granny-woman in order to make the male officers feel comfortable in their world. She tells them, let me take care of the murdered woman, although the autopsy would be done by an entire team of experts. When Crawford uses Starling's gender as an excuse to talk privately to the deputy sheriff to assert his authority, he says there were some details of the sex crime that shouldn't be discussed in front of a woman (80–81). Crawford later apologizes to Starling, saying he just used her to get the deputy sheriff alone, but Starling nonetheless protests: "'It matters, Mr. Crawford. . . . Those cops know who you are. . . . They look at you to see how to act.'" Crawford notes her objection, presumably to act differently the next time (95–96).

As we discussed earlier in this chapter, throughout the novel, Starling is often made uncomfortably aware of her identity as a woman. It is thus ironic that in order to catch Jame Gumb Starling must acknowledge in herself what Gumb "covets" most and what she has willed herself to deny: her own femininity. She tells Crawford that "'I can walk into a woman's room and know three times as much about her as a man would know'" (299). This knowledge helps Starling to recognize the sewing link between Frederica Bimmel and Gumb. But it is also Starling's feminine beauty, particularly her "glorious hair" (346), that delays Gumb's hand when he has her trapped in the dark of his basement.

In "The Philosophy of Composition," Poe remarked on the "circumscription of space" as one of the elements which contributed to the effect of "The Raven." He used the claustrophobic atmosphere of the room in this poem to emphasize the feeling of being trapped which heightened and intensified the pace at which the young man's terror grew. He employed the same device in "Ulalume," in which the narrator unwittingly proceeds through a garden that surrounds and overwhelms him on the anniversary of his love's death.

Poe relies upon a similar use of environment in the detective stories to intensify the atmosphere in which Dupin works. In "The Murders in the Rue Morgue" the women are killed in a locked room. Dupin pays considerable attention to the size of the chamber and to the fact that the windows are nailed shut, all of which provides the reader with a feeling of claustrophobia associated with the room itself. Dupin examines that setting, then retires to his own room to think out the problem. All of the narrative action takes place within enclosed settings, even the moment when Dupin reveals the crime in the sailor's presence. Likewise, in "The Purloined Letter" we again have two enclosed spaces: Dupin's apartment, in which the Prefect describes the problem and where Dupin describes the solution to the narrator, and the Minister's apartment, where the problem is worked out.

In *Silence*, Harris also uses various enclosed chambers, centering on two: Lecter's cell and Gumb's house. Lecter's cell is oppressive because of the masculine threat to Starling, not only from Lecter, but also the other inmates. When Starling enters the prison passageway, she has to run the gauntlet between the cells, making her way down to the end where the only spot of light reveals Lecter. In his presence, she has to keep to the center, remembering not to get too close to the glass, and not to pass any pointed objects to him. Lecter occupies the role of a dragon in the center of the Labyrinth, seemingly waiting to tear her apart and devour her sweet meats.

Lecter's cell is mirrored in Gumb's dungeon-basement. This place is scarier than Lecter's because, while it lacks the energy and powerful threat which Lecter offered (as well as the proximity to armed guards), it is more lifeless. A cold basement, it is a place of denial, limiting food and water to its helpless victim, Catherine Martin. Its cold walls are inhabited only by the echoes of her desperate screams. Harris's detailing of the pit in which she is held captive owes much to Poe's propensity toward drawing a confined bondage of place: "Catherine Martin was free to move around, but there was no place to go. The floor she lay on was oval, about eight by ten feet, with a small drain in the center. It was the bottom of a deep covered pit. The smooth cement walls sloped gently inward as they rose. Sounds from above now or was it her heart?" (154).

This description—the circular prison, the sloping cement walls, the inability to see or hear clearly, and an unseen tormentor—all suggest Harris's close intertextual paralleling to Poe's "The Pit and the Pendulum." As Poe's physical environments reveal information about the interior psychologies of his narrators and their particular compulsions, the construction of Gumb's concrete pit likewise underscores his obsession with the feminine. The walls that slope inward as they rise up from a larger bottom suggest a womb-like structure. Catherine Martin is trapped inside a cement uterus, Gumb's artifical and sterile womb that mirrors his gendered frustration. Martin's isolation is highlighted not only in the sterility of the place itself, but in the very incongruity of its existence: what kind of perverse nature would construct such an environment in the first place, including a huge cement pit in the middle of a suburban basement? And like the narrator of Poe's tale, Catherine is left alone with a single purpose: to cling to sanity even as she is trapped in a microcosm that provokes madness.

There are other enclosed places throughout *Silence*, such as the garage in which Raspail's decapitated body is found. This is even more claustrophobic than Lecter's cell or Gumb's basement because of the lack of room to maneuver. But its effects are more muted because of the outcome. All the objects Starling sees are puzzling; she has been led into the garage by Lecter, but not through it to the mysterious solution of what the head means or why Lecter wants her to discover it. While Starling waits for police reinforcement, the TV reporters arrive. The garage door hides the mystery of Raspail's head, and she lets one cameraman get behind her into the space, which she now has to protect. She lowers the door on him until it touches his chest, bangs on the door, stands on his ankle, and faces the other cameras (55–56). Hair and clothes drenched, standing in the rain, she may not have looked well for her television audience, but she survived—a kind of training for the more complicated and precarious labyrinths that Starling will encounter later in the novel.

In tracing the history of Gothic evolution, Judith Halberstam suggests in her book *Skin Shows* that nineteenth-century monstrosity consisted of a combination of deviant race, class, and gender. In contemporary horror, however, the monster tends, like Buffalo Bill, to demonstrate the markings of a crisis of sexual identity and gendering, but not so much the distinguishing signs of class or race. Halberstam posits that Gumb "is a new kind of sex killer. Buffalo Bill is not interested in getting in women, he never rapes them, he simply wants to get them out of a skin that he perceives to be the essence of femaleness" (168). But Gumb is not the only male who participates in fetish worship over things feminine in this book; all of *Silence*'s men come to appreciate that there is a mystery inherent in the female gender. As we discussed in this chapter's earlier treatment of Starling as feminist detective, there is a unique power inherent in being female in this novel, and the men who encounter this power are, like Chilton, either terrified of it, or, like Lecter and Gumb, covet its special properties.

Gumb is involved in a transcendent process. He cuts gender apart in order to reconfigure it into a suit or uniform that he can use to forge a connection back to his mother and forward to a new and radical gender identity. But as with Poe's monsters, who through early morning hours also dream, eviscerate, and cut in isolation, Gumb's journey is as much a torment as it is a quest for transcendence. The murders of size 14 women bring him no joy, only the knowledge that their deaths are necessary prerequisites to the completion of his task. Until the "woman suit" is finished, Bill remains tortured by *possibility;* his anticipation is hardly balanced by an infernal waiting: "He knows of places, circles, where his efforts would be much admired—there are certain yachts where he could preen—but that will have to wait" (206).

Gumb is trapped in a postmodern gender nightmare. His transgender complications are the consequence, in part, of a quasi-Freudian urge to re-create the image of his mother in himself. More complicated than an Oedipal fixation, Gumb does not wish to possess his mother so much as he wishes to *become* his mother. Prior to each "harvest," Gumb prepares with the ritualized viewing of both his mother's 1948 Miss Sacramento beauty contest videotape and what the son wrongly believes to be her cameo appearance in a pornography film (281–83). Gumb's viewing choices are interesting insofar as they reveal the merging of mother as symbol of purity with the image of woman as seductress, Madonna and Eve, paralleling Gumb's own journey-quest to become both his mother and a desirable sex object. In wearing the skin of the women he kills, Gumb becomes, at least in his own mind, the maternal object he most fears and desires.

Gumb's complex psychosexual transference to, and association with, the feminine is clearly linked to an identification with a lost maternal imago, but his own sexual identity and preferences are not so easily located. Is he a transsexual? A homosexual? Neither or both? In his need to kill the women he wishes to become, Gumb is a modern monster, a creature who defies easy categorization. Hannibal Lecter suggests that "'Billy's not a transsexual, Clarice, but he thinks he is, he tries to be. He's tried to be a lot of things, I expect'" (165). Above all else, Jame Gumb appears to desire change, some sort of physical transformation that will allow for an external expression of his complicated and contradictory internal compulsions. He believes that enacting this transformation is merely a matter of physiological disguise (or assuming the form). As such, Gumb's quest to become female is fueled by his membership in contemporary consumer culture. We learn early that anything is possible in our age of advanced technology. As diet ads, plastic surgery, the fitness industry, and cosmetic makeovers inform us continually, our identities take their shape from whatever physical image our bodies project to the world. In the words of Susan Borgo, we have entered into a "discourse that is gradually changing our conception and experience of our bodies, a discourse that encourages us to 'imagine the possibilities' and close our eyes to limits and consequences" (39). Spirituality and essence are lost in the mirror of corporeal self-recreation; identity and even gender are only skin deep.

Thanks to science, like that of Stevenson's Dr. Jekyll, we have the potential to reshape continually our identities in the refashioning of new bodies. Gumb merely pushes the postmodern invitation to step through the magic mirror of self-transformation to its darkest extreme. And in this context, it is interesting that the image Gumb yearns to assume is that of a female, for women have remained the audience for whom body image makeovers and transformations are primarily directed. And in this context, Harris's novel raises an implicit question: Is Buffalo Bill's choice of particular identity change as much influenced by contemporary fashion advertising as it is by his own compulsion to wear the flesh of women?

In our sympathy for the women victims and Starling's efforts, it is easy to turn Gumb into a grotesque caricature devoid of humanity. But inherent in Gumb's quest to remake his own image is the sad belief that he can escape the destiny of his own corporeality, that he possesses the imagination and technology adequate to the task of self-transformation. The pain of his mother-loss, of his torment as a male, will be wished away in his subterranean fantasy of female construction. In appropriating the feminine form, Gumb seeks to circumvent his own body, pointing the way to a more glamorous world. He has invested his essence in artifice; through his "woman suit" he announces the wish to materialize his imagination through flesh. But with the notable exception of the women victims themselves, who are at least killed before they are flayed, could there be a worse torment than the obvious discrepancy between the interior of Gumb's consciousness—made manifest through painstaking efforts at gender transformation—and the literal embodiment of the being he will actually become? In spite of his best cosmetic efforts, Dr. Frankenstein and his human family are repulsed by the monster's raw corporeality; the reader is gratefully spared the horror of what Gumb would look like wearing his own completed "get-up" (at what points on his body, for instance, would the "woman suit" cut to reveal Gumb himself?). Gumb's dream of refashioning himself as a woman must ultimately leave him in a nether realm where he remains neither male nor female. As a consequence, despite his fantasy projections, the larger world would react to his self-creation with the same spirit of rejection that greeted Frankenstein's creature.

The Silence of the Lambs remains a novel consumed with images of cannibalism: Hannibal the Cannibal, Jame Gumb harvesting human pelts, Jack Crawford's willingness to sacrifice his detectives Starling and Graham, even the manner in which Starling and Lecter ravage each other's minds for information. But the novel itself also cannibalizes the past, specifically the literary past of Poe and the tradition of nineteenth-century Gothicism. Jame Gumb (and, for that matter, Lecter as well) is as much a throwback to the classic monsters of the nineteenth century—the creature created by Dr. Frankenstein, Dracula, and Hyde—as he is a product of postmodern gender distress and our contemporary fascination with the new monster of horror, the serial killer. As we have traced in this chapter, *Silence* borrows heavily from Poe's and Dostoevsky's development of the detective as well as their century's continuing fascination with the Gothic milieu of dungeons, cells, and close enclosures of space. In addition to these elements, however, Harris's novel also creates a unique monster who sutures images of nineteenth-century horror onto the present.

Gumb is as much a victim of his society's restrictive definitions of gender as Stevenson's Dr. Jekyll is a product of middle-class Victorian repression and restraint. In turn, what makes Hyde and Gumb monstrous is that they become outsiders who threaten the values of their respective communities—Hyde by virtue of his ghastly appearance and propensity for violence, Gumb because of his indeterminate sex and gender. Just as Jekyll becomes obsessed with Hyde, hiding him from friends and eventually the law, Buffalo Bill's world is likewise centered on skin which he, too, must conceal in order to maintain his secret project. Hyde is Jekyll's alter ego, a manifestation of his id. The woman that Gumb would become is also an interior creature, an internal imago that must vent itself in physical expression. In both instances, technology makes these transformations feasible: Jekyll relies upon better living through chemistry while Gumb's fantasy form is born through the implementation of a domestic slaughterhouse-factory that features leather-working machines and various chemical agents. (Additionally, at the conclusion of *Silence*, Gumb tracks Starling through his darkened basement with the aid of "masculine technology in the form of infrared binoculars" to give himself an added advantage [Tharp 112].)

Harris's novel also shares interesting parallels with Stevenson's in its narrative design. The narrowing detective investigations that assume central importance in the telling of each of these texts center upon the outside world working its way in. In fact, each narrative moves progressively inward—from the streets of London and the interstate search of the FBI—to the interior "laboratories" of Jekyll and Gumb. By the conclusions of these novels, the outside world has literally and symbolically broken through the doors protecting Jekyll's and Gumb's inner sanctums. However, this narrative action stands in opposition to the psychological design operating in both books, where the inside is shown working its way out (Manlove 5). Jekyll's imagination is overwhelmed by Hyde; Gumb is similarly self-invested in the half-finished hide-vest hanging in his basement. As a consequence, the violent energies locked within each man break out to the point where Hyde engulfs Jekyll while Gumb becomes as much a prisoner to his pelts as their former owners once were to him.

A further connection to Hyde can be seen in Gumb's ambivalence toward women. Gumb believes that becoming female is merely a matter of physiological disguising (or assuming the form); he fails to appreciate that what it means to be female is as much spiritual and psychological as it is physical. Thus, Buffalo Bill's quest to become female is ironically thwarted by the same kind of misogyny that motivates Hyde's treatment of women: under his layers of makeup and flesh, Gumb feels the same scorn for women that we find in Hyde. Recent feminist social theorists, such as Jane Caputi and Robin Morgan, have linked serial sex murderers to the issue of patriarchal abuse. They have argued that both the criminals who perpetrate these crimes, as well as those of us in late capitalist consumer culture who remain fascinated with the details of their perverted acts, are motivated by some of the more sinister aspects of phallocentrism and the fear or hatred of women. In this context, Hyde's omnipresent cane and Gumb's pistol should be seen as phallic tools that are not only employed to hurt women but also signify the male-centered violence of those who use them. Moreover, Gumb's fascination with The Hunt, his sincere regret that he could not prolong the stalking of Starling, is further evidence of his inability to escape a masculinized orientation.

In addition to his connection to Jekyll and Hyde, Buffalo Bill also, as Judith Halberstam reminds us, parallels both Frankenstein and the monster; he is the inventor of new life at the same time as he is the body being re-created, reformed and stitched together. Like Frankenstein, Bill must search abroad for his body parts and return them to his "filthy workshop of creation," and he likewise works alone to the point of obsessional exhaustion. Both men are willing to risk everything for their creations. Harris's monster owes much to Mary Shelley's creature; as we have seen,

Gumb was not born a monster, but was created by his society's reductive definitions of gender, parenting, normalcy, and aesthetic beauty. His rage against the world is fueled by the same sense of social ostracism that motivates Shelley's creature.

In a discussion of contemporary horror fiction, novelist Dan Simmons comments that "so many of horror's characters tend to be Everyman amalgams, two-dimensional stalking horse surrogates for you and me and our fears. In much of modern horror, only the psychopaths and monsters have memorable personalities" (415). Simmons's argument is not merely reflective of modern horror, however; the villains/monsters have *always* been the most interesting figures to shamble out of the two-hundred-year-old Gothic shadows. This stands in sharp opposition to detective tales, in which a detective, the agent of good, is the most memorable personality. This may be partly because the detective often inhabits a series of novels. More central, however, is the form's emphasis on control of the environment, the capturing of the deviant, and the restoration of order with his/her defeat. The desire of detective fiction is not to portray forces destabilizing society, but to rid society of those forces. Ethical enthusiasm takes the detective story to a peaceful, satisfying ending; horror fiction, to an ending disturbed by its reflection of ourselves.

Silence is a novel that stretches and contorts our definition of fundamental constructs: gender, psychoanalysis, cannibalism, concepts of inside and outside, good and evil, the identity of skin itself. Thus, it is not surprising that within this convoluted narrative text, Thomas Harris has sutured the Gothic tale to the detective story and created a hybrid that embodies the most important elements of each genre. The novel manages to terrify at the same time as it reassures. Its monsters surely represent Simmons's "memorable personalities" of serial killer, gender bender, cultured cannibal, and avatar to the nineteenth century. Its feminist detective, on the other hand, is both an "Everywoman amalgam" and a character who gradually comes to cultivate Dupin's intuitive capabilities.

Chapter 6
The Overlook Hotel and Beyond:
Stephen King as Poe's Postmodern Heir

Q: Do you feel as if you're part of a tradition, and if so, who are the other members of that tradition?

KING: I feel that way very much. I discovered Poe when I was in grammar school, and from Poe I went on and discovered people like Ambrose Bierce and H. P. Lovecraft. Those people played a part in teaching me how to write, and they also made it possible for me to make a living. (Underwood and Miller 116)

While perusing a scrapbook containing selected illustrations of decadence and greed from the past history of the Overlook Hotel, Jack Torrance, the protagonist in Stephen King's 1977 novel *The Shining*, interrupts himself with the first of the novel's many allusions to Poe's "Masque of the Red Death." After examining an invitation to a Masked Ball held at the hotel in 1945, Torrance is motivated to recall the last line of Poe's tale: *"The Red Death held sway over all!"* The many intertextual relationships between Torrance's discovery of the Overlook's past and Poe's short tale of power and selfishness will be a focus of commentary later in this chapter. But for now, let us consider Jack Torrance's personal reaction to this Poe allusion: "He frowned. What left field had that come out of? That was Poe, the Great American Hack. And surely the Overlook—this shining, glowing Overlook on the invitation he held in his hands—was the farthest cry from E. A. Poe imaginable" (157).

If Edgar Poe has attained the status of a popular icon in contemporary American culture—"the Great American Hack"—then what are we to call Stephen King himself? At this writing, twenty-one of King's books have made the *New York Times* best-seller list. At one point in 1987, it was rumored in the publishing world that one out of every four books being printed had Stephen King's name on the title page (Carroll 207). It is no exaggeration to assert that Stephen King has become America's story-teller; he is a remarkable and singular phenomenon in the history of American publishing. His record-breaking advances and saturation distribution—with nearly 250 million books in circulation—have made his name, no less than Poe's, a household commodity. As Clive Barker has noted, "There are apparently two books in every American household—one of them is the Bible, and the other one is probably by Stephen King" (Skal 17).

Since Poe's tragic death in 1849, he has, in essence, become an object of mass consumption by the very culture that once ignored him, and whose "mob mentality" was so often vilified in several of Poe's harshest parodies. All of Poe's fictionalized encounters with the democratic society he simultaneously solicited and scorned, suggest that he could be both involved and critical of contemporary popular sentiments and opinions. In tracing Poe's relationship with American mass culture of his own time and ours, Jonathan Elmer speculates that "Poe's work, in both its subject matter and its execution, may be more closely allied with a popular, nonserious, or mass culture than with the 'highest' artistic achievements" (4). Certainly, Poe's fascination with the various fads and scientific expeditions of his time—journeys to the center of the earth via the North Pole, transatlantic balloons, cryptnography, crime stories from home and abroad, and the varied subjects he culled from his extensive reading of periodicals he both worked for and competed against—fueled the fiction that was pure hoax, such as "The Balloon Hoax," as well as those tales, such as "The Mystery of Marie Roget," that were fictionalized adaptations based upon actual and unsolved crimes. In short, Poe was a product of his era, utilizing in the creation of his work both popular culture and historical events, even though Poe scholars, until recently, have tended to read his fiction as though it were produced in an ahistorical vacuum.

King's incredible financial success sometimes belies the influence he has had upon the very culture that created him. Through the books and many film adaptations that have been made of his fiction, Stephen King has become that rare example of an artist who not only manages to capture into his art something essential about his particular time and place, but has likewise managed to exert a profound influence over the culture itself. Indeed, in terms of the horror market alone, Stephen King's presence for the past two and a half decades has literally dominated the shelves of bookstores across America, mainstreaming and legitimizing a genre that was once relegated to specialty bookshops and basement closets. Equally as important, his success has inspired other writers to enter into the field, induced Hollywood to produce more horror films based largely on the success of the cinematic adaptation of King's work (as of this writing, no film made from a Stephen King narrative has failed to turn a profit), and persuaded readers and filmgoers alike to seek out the range of work available in this genre. It is no coincidence that King now rivals Edgar Poe as a favorite topic for high school term papers and reports. Moreover, it is probably fair to assume that the admonishments of English teachers all across the Western world notwithstanding, Stephen King is currently shaping an entire generation of neophyte fiction writers as well as readers, just as Poe has done for successive generations for the past century and a half.

As in Poe's best tales, King's most successful work has always been plot-driven. Both writers share an understanding that for horror to operate on its most effective plane it must describe a situation that is terrifying because it is life-threatening. Characters in their canons are recognizable human beings who have, in most cases, been pushed to psychological extremes. The obsessive natures of Poe's male protagonists certainly find parallels in *The Shining*'s Jack Torrance and *Pet Sematary*'s Louis Creed. But perhaps the most important comparison that must be made between Poe and King is that both employ the tale of terror as a means for highlighting human frailties, unhealthy psychological conditions, and the potentially self-destructive situations that are the consequences of poor choices and the cruelty of fate. King shares with Poe the ability to do more than shock or thrill readers; their art disturbs so thoroughly because in their respective protagonists we recognize our own darkest propensities and worst inclinations. King's immense popularity, like Poe's, is due in no small measure to his ability to write about characters with whom most of us can identify.

As we traced in Chapters 1 and 2, Poe was the first writer to press the interpersonal connections between acts of terror and mayhem and the reader to the point where this relationship becomes simultaneously unbearable and impossible to resist. And as we have also seen, this perverse identification with deviant psychology is critical to the relationship forged between Dupin and the criminal in his detective tales as well. There are certain darkly obsessed figures that also keep reappearing in King's fictional microcosm as well, and we will turn to them later in this chapter, for they share a dark brotherhood with many of Poe's protagonists. But King is finally a more hopeful artist than was Poe. As Mark Edmundson notes in his book, *Nightmare on Main Street*, "Unlike Poe, who thinks that humans are mostly damned and doomed from the start, Rousseauian King sees evil as something that gets added on, a product of socialization in a bad world" (45). If we are to explain fully the phenomenal popular attraction that he continues to exert around the world, we must consider the role of the hero in Stephen King's microcosm, a privileged status that is noticeably absent throughout the whole of Poe's canon.

Up until the more recent publications of *Gerald's Game* (1992), *Dolores Claiborne* (1993), and *Rose Madder* (1995), the hero figure in Stephen King was usually from the white, male middle class, a common man, exemplified in characters such as Stuart Redman in *The Stand* (1978) or John Smith in *The Dead Zone* (1979). These individuals find themselves in situations where their ordinary lives have become suddenly extraordinary. What King appears most interested in testing in *The Dead Zone* and *The Stand* is the mettle of these ordinary characters faced with extraordinary circumstances, watching them struggle and become greater than they ever thought they were capable of becoming. Until the 1990s, King's landscape was populated almost exclusively with heroes rather than heroines. In *Gerald's Game, Rose Madder*, and *Dolores Claiborne*, however, King expands the center of his fictional universe to include women. Yet even these feminist characterizations also adhere to the heroic template defined above. While King's fiction mirrors an American, particularly a *New England* American, distrust of institutions and governmental bureaucracy, he also sees a fundamental resiliency in the human spirit. In his tales of terror, as in Poe's tales of detection, the individual is of supreme importance, and he or she will survive and endure. But the institutions that individuals put together—from small town communities to the United States government itself—are unsavory and unholy places in Stephen King's world. This is a writer who is far less committed to the politics of reinventing community than he is interested in exploring the timeless moral issues that are inherent within individual choices. And because he believes deeply in the individual's ability to rise above both the terror and potentially tragic situations that often confront him or her, King ultimately supplies an element of reassurance to a contemporary audience that perceives itself under constant assault.

King's fiction is a carefully drawn, immediately recognizable world. He is most at home not in the exotic milieu of Poe's perfumed antechambers or decadent mansions; instead, King has rendered a vivid portrait of middle-class American life in the latter half of the twentieth century. That this portrait can often appear as psychologically distorted as Poe's, is still to be considered; but, clearly, as Thomas Tessier points out, King also provides middle-class America a mirrored reflection of itself: "He is the scribe of the baby boomers and, to a certain extent, their kids. King *knows* childhood in the fifties, adolescence in the sixties, maturing and settling down in the seventies. This is what he offers his audience, in the form of hundreds of memories, echoes, pictures, and names. Forget the melodrama and the varying frights; what's really happening is that King is holding up a mirror to his generation. They see themselves and for the most part they like what they see" (76).

This is an accurate approach to defining the demographics of King's popular audience, but it does little by way of supplying much insight into what makes King attractive to an academic audience. While King has not yet achieved the respectability afforded Poe in the academy, it is also possible to argue that no other best-selling author in contemporary American fiction has come close to attracting the depth of scrutiny or breadth of critical attention afforded Stephen King. Just as we have examined Poe as a seminal figure that connects popular culture and academic scholarship, Stephen King continues to interest a dedicated body of scholarly interpreters in addition to his large and broad-based popular audience. At this writing, a quick name search of "Stephen King" in the *MLA Bibliography* database turned up over 140 books, journal articles, and dissertations referencing King. And the critical approaches that are used in interpreting his work are as extensive as for any other site of academic study: feminist and gender-based readings, psychoanalytic analyses (both Freudian and Jungian), historical and regional emphases, Bakhtinian, Marxist, and postmodernist contexts, even examinations of the racial and ethnic subtexts of his fiction.

Literary critic Brian Kent supplies a helpful starting point for this discussion: "King has carved out a sizable audience of scholarly-academic readers, while maintaining and expanding his massive popular appeal. For while his heart may be with that huge popular audience, his mind often lands him in academic terrain, in terms of his own awareness of the standards and skills around which university English departments cohere" (40). It is not just King's "standards and skills," however, that must be cited as a reason for the critical attention that has centered on his work. At its best, these scholarly enterprises often focus not upon Tessier's benign portrait of middle-class nostalgia and sentiment, but rather the serious flaws inherent in an America that King portrays to be on the verge of destroying itself internally (in terms of its moral lapses) and externally (in terms of environmental disasters and the bankruptcy of its social institutions).

As Poe projected the anxieties of democracy into his tales of terror, King's skill in exploring and revealing the traditional phobias of horror fiction dovetails into the current sense of vulnerability that Americans feel in the "collapse of the American Empire and the culture of the indomitable individual that it was supposed to guarantee" (Carroll 213). No literature, not even the literature of the fantastic, can be understood as discrete from the culture out of which it arises. Behind the supernatural inclusion of vampires and other Gothic monsters, which remains one of the great popular attractions of his fiction, King's world mirrors our own. Each of his novels and many of the stories feature at least one individual who suffers from some type of addictive behavior. Liquor, cocaine, heroin, Valium, Norvil, and perverted sexuality are the drugs that numb the consciousnesses of so many King characters; their abuse suggests all the symptoms of social decay and all the modes of self-destruction that flourish, largely tolerated, in our society.

Most of Stephen King's readers are unconscious of, or perhaps even uninterested in, the socio-political dimensions of his fiction. He is, after all, a writer of fantastic tales, and the genre tends to veil social subtexts beneath the veneer of supernatural horror. A similar argument is often raised in discussing Edgar Poe's orientation toward America in the 1830s and 1840s. Since F. O. Matthiessen deliberately excluded Poe from his seminal study *American Renaissance* (1941) because Poe did not conform to a sufficiently ideological strain necessary for inclusion into Matthiessen's paradigm, scholars have tended to read Poe as a visionary operating outside the realm of politics and history. But recent Poe criticism has endeavored to place the writer in cultural contexts; David Leverenz's "Poe and Gentry Virginia" and Joan Dayan's "Amorous Bondage: Poe, Ladies, and Slaves," for example, explore Poe's manipulation of the real and mythological aspects of the nineteenth-century southern gentleman, particularly insofar as it shaped Poe's attitude toward women and blacks.

In any event, it seems impossible not to read Poe as somehow commenting upon his epoch, even when the writer appears most disengaged from American culture. In an age where America's literary and national voices were shaped by Emersonian transcendentalism and its belief in self-reliance and an expansionist philosophy, Poe offered a constant rebuttal in asserting that Americans were essentially no different, better or worse, than people of any other culture at any other point in history. With his emphasis upon a circumscribed Gothic landscape filled with terror and decay, Poe countered the transcendental hopefulness that dominated his age. Throughout his career, Poe, like Melville and Hawthorne, was severely critical of Emerson's nebulous metaphysics, democratic spirit, and transcendental pontifications. In distinguishing between what he has delineated as the two dominant strains of American poetry, the legacy of Whitman versus that of Poe, critic Leslie Fiedler argues that the populist Whitmanian represents the essence of the American ideal and speaks directly to the American masses. In contrast, no writer derived from the tradition that Poe established can be labeled patriotic, for his art is a consequence of what he finds wrong with America (200). The Whitman ideal is always stressed in terms of a relationship among the masses; for Poe, it is the individual who is at the center of the poem or horror story, his loneliness and alienation go without relief.

While Stephen King appears to harbor strong democratic feelings for working men and women, particularly New England men and women, Poe was confessedly anti-democratic. King, however, is a child of Watergate and Vietnam, and his criticism directed at the American government and its institutions bear strong similarities to Poe's attitude toward the government of his own time as "the most odious and insupportable despotism . . . upon the face of the earth" (Van Doren Stern xxxv). In his poems and narrative fictions, far more than his cosmological treatises, Poe believed that we inhabit a universe unfavorably disposed toward humankind, and that human nature itself was simply untrustworthy. Indeed, as the America of the 1840s looked brightly into a future of limitless possibilities, Poe's work, no less than Stephen King's a century and a half later, counterpointed the general spirit of American optimism in revealing the human propensity to seek pain rather than pleasure, decay rather than growth, terror rather than tranquility.

Edgar Poe's popularity has maintained itself in spite of the fact that he remains one of the more complex and allusive writers in all of American literature. His knowledge of classical languages and obscure philosophical texts is often cited to enrich and deepen the meanings of individual works. Relying upon the cosmological philosophers and astronomers of his time, especially Pierre Simon Marquis de Laplace and Friedrich Heinrich Alexander Baron von Humboldt, author of *The Cosmos*, Poe constructed, in his 1848 treatise entitled *Eureka: A Prose Poem*, a cosmological synthesis based upon mathematics, poetics, and intuition. His knowledge of Shakespeare in "Masque of the Red Death," to reference merely one of the more obvious examples, extends beyond Prospero's character and name to the very concept for the story itself, in which Prospero is cut off from the rest of the world in Shakespeare's *The Tempest*. In short, Poe's knowledge of philosophy, literature, music, and art history have been the subjects of a myriad of scholarly journal articles, books, and Ph.D. dissertations for more than a century. Yet his high cultural reputation has in no way distracted the popular appeal of his fiction, nor, on the other hand, has his popularity diminished the central importance of his legacy to the mainstream literatures of France, Russia, and, of course, the United States.

As the self-proclaimed literary equivalent of a meal at McDonald's, Stephen King would seem to possess the literary pedigree of a mongrel when compared to Poe's pure breeding. And for better than two decades this has been a primary justification for many academicians to relegate King's work to the redundant efforts of supermarket authors such as Danielle Steel and John Grisham. But King's corpus is not so easily dismissed. While his fiction does possess, as we have seen, a strong mass attraction, this does not necessarily mean that it is unsophisticated, unliterary, or even unscholarly. King's knowledge and use of literary allusions is surely no less relevant than Poe's; the fullest appreciation of both artists requires a certain awareness of the sourcework they draw upon. And while King's books certainly reflect the dominance of a distinctly American literary legacy, he has chosen his mentors carefully and well. Mary Jane Dickerson and Jeanne Campbell Reesman, for example, have both traced the influence of William Faulkner, one of King's favorite writers, on the novel *IT* Tony Magistrale has established close lines of contact between *Pet Sematary* and the fiction of Nathaniel Hawthorne. Other literary critics have argued that King shares numerous literary parallels with writers as diverse as Ernest Hemingway and William Carlos Williams. It remains for scholars to continue to explore the intertextual relationships that Stephen King readily acknowledges to many of the mainstream authors (and several of the lesser known ones as well) in the American canon. But any discussion of the influences that have shaped Stephen King's vision over the years must eventually circle back to Poe. For Poe is an artist who has constantly inspired the shape of King's universe, and this is evident both in terms of the direct frequency of citations to various Poe works and in the resonance of meaning that Poe has supplied King's fiction.

One of the devices King derives from Poe is the difference between the way horror and detective fiction employ revelation and transformation of character. The more stable detective fiction has characters already determined by the beginning of the tale: the process of detection strips off layer after layer of deception to reveal the murderer, as well as other miscreants, whose crimes were committed before the tale began. Instead of observing character development, the reader's knowledge and perceptions of character change. The horror tale features characters that transform monstrously; detective fiction focuses on the revelation of monstrous behavior that has already occurred.

The dynamic of horror fiction features characters who are more fluid, shape changers. The hero of "The Black Cat," for example, is at first a kind man, loving his wife, other pets, and his black cat. But he falls under the spell of alcohol and turns from what he says he is, a man in the midst of "mere household events," (199) into the monster who cuts out his cat's eye with a penknife, hangs the cat from a tree in the yard, murders his wife with an axe, and entombs her and the cat into the cellar wall. In the same way, the narrator of "The Tell-Tale Heart" first loves the old man, then grows to hate him, his hate focusing on the eye, then kills him, dismembers him, and buries his body under the floorboards. And then, it is his own change in character which causes him to break down and confess to his crime. A detective story would have begun with the murder already committed and traced the detective's deduction of who killed the old man. The characters would already be fixed; what would change would be our knowledge of the character.

The Shining's Jack Torrance is similarly transformed from loving father into shuffling monster, wielding a roque mallet as it shows the last vestiges of fatherly love in advising Danny to run away. Jack is transformed into the "Hyde" part of himself that was always there, but consciously repressed. Since he is sincere in his role as a loving husband and father, his dark depths were hidden even from himself. The murderer in the detective story is always aware of the crime he has committed and does his best to misdirect both police and detective. In the course of King's novel, Jack moves into a role similar to that of the criminal in a detective novel. As his allegiance to the hotel grows, his need to hide his guilt and association with the Overlook's ghosts results in behavior that is deceptive and destructive: he refrains from revealing his knowledge of the playground as a dangerous place for Danny to play, he smashes the hotel's radio, incapacitates the snowmobile. As he comes to assume more criminal traits, he correspondingly relinquishes both his sincerity and his familial responsibilities.

While Danny, Wendy, and Hallorann grow more mature from their battle against evil, discovering sources of inner strength that they did not believe they actually possessed, Jack does not grow but instead regresses—back to his father, on the one hand, but also to some primal beast nearly incoherent with rage. He always possessed traits of weakness that the hotel could exploit within himself. He has always been a caretaker, but initially it was of his family, only later does it become the hotel. And it is only with the destruction of the hotel that Jack's identity is destroyed and he is changed completely into the monster.

As a work of the imagination, *The Shining*, more than any other King narrative, reverberates with echoes from different pasts. The history of the Overlook Hotel, the twentieth-century legacy of American violence and corruption, the abusive relationships as children that Wendy and Jack Torrance struggle to avoid repeating as adults, and Jack's history of alcoholism and dysfunctional behavior are central elements that determine the novel's blurring of unique temporal times and individual histories. One of the most impressive aspects of *The Shining* is its ability to juxtapose all these different pasts into a nightmarish present. It is therefore no mere coincidence that Jack Torrance should provide the first allusion to Edgar Poe and his short story "The Masque of the Red Death"—a tale whose meaning will reverberate down the empty corridors and through the stately ballrooms of the Overlook for the remainder of the novel—at the very moment he discovers the scrapbook in Chapter 18. As a record of the Overlook's secret and public histories, the scrapbook represents a critical component in establishing the weight of the past as a burden that simultaneously excites and dooms Jack Torrance. Just as the scrapbook becomes a major distraction for Jack, Poe and his short story complicate Torrance's connection to the Overlook and its infamous parties. The Poe reference provides yet another layer of mystery and meaning to the Overlook's already complex history.

Like Prince Prospero, sequestered inside a fortress that eventually becomes both prison and tomb, Torrance is haunted by his own past, the Hotel's, and, finally, by Poe himself. Clearly Prospero shares much in common with King's protagonist: they are both supremely selfish men consumed with their own worldly success and social status. Deliberately entombing himself and a select group of citizens to avoid the plague, the

Prince creates a decadent milieu where "There were much of the beautiful, much of the wanton, much of the *bizarre*, something of the terrible, and not a little of that which might have excited disgust" (177). In this self-enclosed microcosm, Prospero remains oblivious to the suffering of his dominion and subjects, "The Prince Prospero was happy and dauntless and sagacious . . . . The external world could take care of itself" (175). Prospero creates a "voluptuous scene" (175) that is echoed in the allure of King's hotel. Party Central for "the richest men in America and their women" (157), the Overlook's guests are similarly self-absorbed, concerned exclusively with their own pleasures; they too wear masks that separate them from less fortunate men and women and what moral responsibility exists for the care and maintainance of others. In both worlds, perhaps reflecting the inevitable consequences of too much money and power, there is an omnipresent admixture of beauty and disgust.

The Overlook's eras of prestige and opulence seduce Jack because he is a man who is in desperate search of something to believe in personally—a success story of his own. As a fallen man himself, Jack has as much in common with the Overlook as any of its ghosts or living allies. Almost from the moment he begins reading about it, Jack feels a unique affinity with the place. But the discerning reader of *The Shining* also comes to recognize that Torrance is not merely intrigued by the history he discovers in the scrapbook; he is wholly absorbed by it. He wants to research the details, to write and publish them, to attain an intimate oneness with their reality. Between its covers, Torrance finds a melange of newspapers, letters, photographs, and seemingly random notations that detail events from the hotel's nefarious history. It is as if the Overlook is filling the darkest chambers of Torrance's mind with details of its darkest moments in history while he sits alone reading in a corner of its darkest room. As Torrance comes to replace his family and his writing career with the Overlook itself, he is transformed into an active agent for the hotel, tied to an important place with "serious responsibilities" that stretch beyond the mundane realm of family and work. If Torrance cannot quite envision himself as Poe's Prince, he yearns secretly at least to be one of the invited "hale and light-hearted friends . . . retired to the deep seclusion of his castellated abbeys" (175). By the end of the novel, he gets his wish: like the forever-sequestered knights and ladies who constitute Prospero's doomed revelers, Torrance joins the Overlook's permanent guest registry.

Poe's influence on *The Shining* is most discernible in King's use of characterization and setting as Poe provides rich analogies and allusions of which King is always consciously aware. But there is another, more subtle way that the nineteenth-century writer haunts this fiction. *The Shining* is a novel of ghosts, history, and a nuclear family under siege. It is also a story of alcoholism. King manages to capture all of the most important details associated with this disease: from the manner in which those individuals closest to the alcoholic are affected by his behavior to the lingering guilt and psychic vulnerability that come with the choice of abstinence. In the writing of this book, Stephen King saddled his protagonist with many of the real-life problems he himself had encountered prior to the swift success that attended the sale of the paperback rights to *Carrie* in 1975: his fear of never making a living as a writer (*The Shining* became King's first hardcover bestseller in 1977), his anxiety at suddenly becoming the breadwinner for a young family, his difficulties with early parenthood, and his tendency to turn to alcohol as a means of escape. In describing these circumstances in an interview with *Playboy*, King's description of these fledgling years bears an interesting relationship to Jack Torrance's situation in Colorado, particularly in terms of its encroaching financial desperation and ever-present threat of self-annihilation:

> "We were as poor as church mice, with two small kids, and needless to say, it wasn't easy to make ends meet on that salary [teaching English at a prep school and working in an industrial laundry]. I'd come home exhausted from school and squat in the trailer's furnace room, with Tabby's little Olivetti portable perched on a child's desk I had to balance on my knees, and try to hammer out some scintillating prose . . . . Anyway, the payment for my stories wasn't enough to keep us out of the red, and I was getting nowhere with my longer work. My kids were wearing hand-me-downs from friends and relatives, our old rattletrap 1965 Buick Special was rapidly self-destructing and we finally had to ask Ma Bell to remove our phone. On top of everything else, I was fucking up personally. I wish I could say today that I bravely shook my fist in the face of adversity and carried on undaunted, but I can't. I copped out to self-pity and anxiety and started drinking far too much and frittering money away on poker and bumper pool. (Underwood and Miller 30–31)

While it is clear from this statement that King included many autobiographical details in shaping *The Shining*, what is less immediately apparent is that this self-revelation also shares an uncanny number of parallels to the career of Edgar Allan Poe. While an undergraduate at the University of Virginia, Poe took up gambling to obtain money that his foster father, John Allan, refused to send him. As he lost greater amounts of money, he continued to wager still more. During these early years of financial struggle, Poe initiated what would become a life-long problem with alcohol. He tried on several occasions to give up drinking—his letters attest poignantly to his efforts—but was never able to free himself. He established a pattern similar to the one Jack Torrance follows in *The Shining*: extended periods of time away from drunkenness, followed inevitably by the urge to seek release from intolerable circumstances with just one drink, and then the relapse into public intoxication and boorish conduct. Economic desperation compounded by domestic crises were among the demons with which Poe was forced to contend on a daily basis. And like Torrance, Poe's penchant for self-pity and argumentiveness was exacerbated each time he turned to alcohol. On more than one occasion, his alcoholic behavior cost him jobs and friendships.

In the end, Jack Torrance comes to share more in common with Edgar Poe than he does with his creator, Stephen King. King emerged from his early penury to become the famous author that Torrance could only dream of someday becoming himself. And while Stephen King has learned to regulate his predilection toward substance abuse, alcohol only pushed Poe and Torrance further from reality and toward their ultimate isolation in death. Poe's ill-fated life began, as did Jack Torrence's, with an unstable family background, and for both this instability, particularly in their mutual antagonism toward paternal authority, never totally resolved itself. As King has noted, "Jack Torrance himself is a haunted house. He's haunted by his father. It pops up again and again and again" (Underwood and Miller 105). In Poe's case, his relationship with John Allan, his guardian and foster father, was a saga of mounting mutual dislike that gradually deepened into permanent animosity with distinct overtones of violence. Poe may well have recreated his foster father in his fictional portrayals of dark fathers and judgmental authority figures; his lifelong resentment of paternal authority can be heard, for example, in the lament from the narrator of his last poem, "Annabel Lee": "So that her highborn kinsmen came and bore her away from me."

King's paternal figures are seldom more sympathetic than what we discover in Poe. Just as Poe was orphaned at an early age, King's own father, Donald, left the King family when Stephen was two years old. Donald was never seen or heard from again by his family. As the absence of a positive father in his life may have shaped Poe's attitude toward creating fictional fathers, perhaps the best that can be said about the patriarchs in King's universe is that they, like the grieving father in *The Body*, possess a benign indifference toward their offspring and spouse. Unfortunately, the majority resemble more the Torrance men: destructively active presences that are inflamed by alcohol and barely capable of masking their propensity toward violence and sexual degeneracy. Indeed, King's most treacherous formulations of sin, and certainly their most pervasive designs, are male-generated and sustained. From the carefully-guarded episodes of incestual abuse in *IT, Gerald's Game* and *Dolores Claiborne*, to the perverted father-son bond that develops between an ex-Nazi and a precocious American boy in *Apt Pupil*, to the patriarchal partnership that eventually destroys the lives and families of Jud Crandall and Louis Creed in *Pet Sematary*, King's portrayal of evil most often appears to require an active, illicit bond between a male (often in the role of a father or father surrogate) and a younger, formerly innocent individual (often in the role of biological daughter or surrogate son) who is initiated into sin. Jack Torrance's decision to align himself with his father signals his doom. And this is a familial pattern that is repeated throughout King's canon: an unspoken collusion between fathers and (surrogate) children that upholds some kind of dark, secret covenant.

King not only shares Poe's psychological orientation toward character, he also inherited the latter's obsessional awareness of a psychology of place. The Overlook Hotel is animated with the same supernatural biology that we find in Poe's House of Usher and the ever-transforming hellish dreamscape of "The Pit and the Pendulum." The Overlook Hotel is the ultimate embodiment of the haunted house tradition as it was first established in the European Gothic castle and later embellished in Poe's American landscape. But in addition to being modeled upon these progenitor literary texts, the Overlook does its sourcework one better: it goes on to absorb them, so that Jack Torrance, as well as the literate reader, never fully emerges from shadows cast by Poe's haunted places.

In addition to the intertextual link between Prospero's pleasure palace and the Overlook itself, both literary works also feature clocks that signal important commentary upon the respective temporal realities of each narrative. Douglas Winter asserts that "the mystery of the Overlook is one of time. In the hotel, as in Prince Prospero's castle, time stops with the stroke of midnight, suggesting that the future, like the past, is already determined" (51). In "The Masque of the Red Death," Poe employs an ebony clock to underscore the appearance of the plague at midnight. The clock symbolizes the end of Prospero's reign and the demise of his efforts to circumvent death's inevitability. In *The Shining*, the wind-up clock that Danny sets in motion in Chapter 37 subverts linear time, forcing Overlook past and present into an unholy juxtaposition. As Leonard Mustazza points out, the clock in "Masque" plays a "large role in the dark pessimism of Poe's story," since the plague itself and the chiming of the clock are linked to underscore the doom of man. *The Shining* also uses the clock to highlight "the idea of time's pernicious effects" (111). Danny sets the clock, and by extension, the hotel itself, into motion. In this way, *The Shining* appears to embody some of the deterministic features that characterize Poe's tale, as once Danny brings this machinery to life, he is helpless to stop it. Both these texts use clocks and time to underscore an essential Gothic premise: that the past is the most active agent in a Gothic fiction, rising up to devour any attempt to avoid or reshape it.

King's debt to Poe's presence in *The Shining* is notable on so many levels that the comparison alone could easily occupy the remainder of this entire chapter. Such a definitive treatment would certainly be appropriate, but it is not our only purpose here, for there are other King tales that also reflect Poe's tutelage. While they may not possess the intertextual richness afforded *The Shining*, these narratives deepen our understanding of the range of influence that Poe continues to exert on King's work.

As we have seen in *The Shining*, it is apparent that King often creates parallels to Poe's narratives in both character and plot. "Dolan's Cadillac," from the collection *Nightmares and Dreamscapes*, addresses the same issue that informs "The Cask of Amontillado": Is the urge for revenge worth the madness that attends such an obsession? As in Poe's narrative, the reader of King's tale of elaborate revenge modernized is drawn into the restricted world of Robinson, the story's protagonist. He readies a trap for a gangster boss named Dolan, the man responsible for the murder of the narrator's wife. Like Poe's Montressor, he takes great pride in the design of his revenge; but King attempts to do Poe's artful *tour de force* one better: Dolan is not only buried alive, his car becomes his coffin and a stretch of Nevada interstate his tomb.

What is handled most efficiently in this tale is King's use of first-person narration. In her relationship with Montressor, the reader ends up participating vicariously in the act of revenge: she is made to witness each brick stacked into the wall of "Amontillado"; in King's story we are likewise drawn into Robinson's obsessional world, made to experience the effects of sunstroke, to feel the grit of the asphalt as it is sectioned, dug out, and then replaced, piece by piece. As a result of his loss, Robinson has allowed himself to become a man possessed; his dead wife exerts such a presence over his need for revenge that her voice fills his head with words of encouragement. Although we are informed that she is silenced after the death of Dolan, the narrator—and here he resembles Poe's Montressor most completely—still feels driven to relive the experience by narrating it in exquisite detail to his audience. The abbreviated requiem of the jingling of the bells at the end of Poe's tale is echoed in Dolan's wild pistol shots from inside the prized cadillac fortress that has now become his tomb. Even Poe's mock epitaph, "Yes, for the love of God" is repeated by Robinson in answer to Dolan's final plea for mercy. His revenge becomes as much a marker for Robinson's life as it is for Montressor's fifty years later; both men are compelled to return to the retelling of their stories, and they appear somehow comforted in each memorial reenactment.

As we have seen throughout this chapter, King possesses a profound awareness of his place as part of a literary tradition that is richly bifurcated between the European Gothic and nineteenth and twentieth-century American literature. But just as often, he has acknowledged his debt to less mainstream, popular writers, specifically and most interestingly to the concerns of this book, detective novelists such as Ed McBain, John D. MacDonald, Arthur Conan Doyle, and Dashiell Hammett (Underwood and Miller 78, 123, 135). This connection might appear initially surprising, as King is seldom associated with the detective genre. But a more careful consideration reveals that the standard detective mystery does much to shape fictions such as *The Dark Half, The Shawshank Redemption, Needful Things* and *Dolores Claiborne*. These books all share in common the slow revelation of criminality and the eventual disclosure of criminal behavior that has gone unpunished. While actual detectives are present only in *The Dark Half, Needful Things* and *Dolores Claiborne*, the heroes and heroines in all of these novels occupy roles analogous to that of the typical detective: helping to piece together evidence of past crimes that continue to haunt and confuse their present lives. As these characters gain insight into criminal activity that has often been attributed to them unjustly, the truth is revealed, their own innocence is reaffirmed, and evil is appropriately vanquished.

Perhaps the closest figure to C. Auguste Dupin that King has yet formulated is the sheriff Alan Pangborn, who appears in *Needful Things* and *The Dark Half*. Similar to Sherlock Holmes (a character King has publicly admired on several separate occasions) and many of the other detectives we have referenced in this book, Pangborn distinguishes himself from the afflicted townspeople of each respective novel—the gamblers, the sexually perverse, the amoral, the men most prone to violence, the walking dead who have sacrificed their reason, vision, and morality. Patient, imaginative, and capable of employing a Dupin-like understanding that the extraordinary always manifests itself in the ordinary, he is one of the last moral men who struggles against the seductive powers of evil and debasement. In both novels, Pangborn appears as a final barrier between justice and corruption, society's enduring values and its wholesale ethical destruction. King's detective, then, is closely aligned to the other moral heroes and heroines who populate his canon. Isolated as a result of an ethical estrangement that separates him from the negative psyche that engulfs the community of Castle Rock, his unselfish dedication to other people and the pursuit of justice supplies a venue for both personal and social survival.

As we noted in Chapter 1, one of Poe's recurrent themes in most of his major tales is the double, or split self. The concept of a second self, of an unrestrained other loosed upon the world and living within ourselves, is also a major preoccupation for Stephen King. We can trace the development of the double throughout a novel such as *The Dark Half*, but it is also clear that King's authorial pseudonym—Richard Bachman—has supplied the writer with a necessary alter ego for the release of some of King's own literary demons. The novels published under Bachman's name permitted King to indulge his worst fantasies and speculations. This is not to argue that Bachman's vision is somehow separate from King's, but the Bachman work is best interpreted as representing a pessimistic side of King's psyche. Bachman remains unmoved by the power of love, the force that absolutely inspires King's most persuasive fiction. Yet the Bachman novels were written by the mind that also produced Randall Flagg and Annie Wilkes—a mind which understands intimately the nihilistic impulse. If Bachman can be seen as King's William Wilson-like writing alter ego, their relationship forms an intriguing parallel to that between George Stark and his creator, Thad Beaumont, in *The Dark Half*. In both instances the pseudonym functions as a dark (but apparently necessary) double for the artist, an avenue for venting his most violent and pessimistic inclinations.

As in "William Wilson," Beaumont struggles to deny his relationship with Stark. In fact, Stark has his origins in Beaumont's psyche, literally and metaphorically. He is Beaumont's fetal twin as well as an extension of the writer's psychological id. Beaumont has not only indulged his darkest urges in writing Stark's fiction; he has also profited financially from his popularity. However, while Beaumont lives a contented middle-class life with wife and children, Stark's status remains that of street punk whose actions are violent and opposed to the normal world Beaumont inhabits. As in Poe's "William Wilson," King's novel highlights the differences between these two alter egos. The action of both narratives turns self-destructive when an attempt is made to disrupt the uneasy balance of their relationship by eliminating one of the principles.

The only Poe poem that has found its way into King's canon to date is "The Raven," but its themes of isolation and loss reverberate through several King texts, most notably the 1992 novel *Gerald's Game*. Much as the language "Unmask!" and "The Red Death held illimitable dominion over all" (180) is repeated throughout *The Shining*, Poe's famous "Nevermore." is the omnipresent refrain that holds dominion over Jessie Burlingame's situation and consciousness in *Gerald's Game*. And just as these references to "The Masque of the Red Death" are meant to deepen the meaning of *The Shining*, in *Gerald's Game* the allusion to "The Raven" underscores the self-induced "psychological bondage" that has plagued Jessie for years prior to Gerald's interest in tying her arms to the bedposts. While engaging in an afternoon's alternative sex play with her husband, she unwittingly uncovers a connection between Gerald's need to dominate her and an incestual incident that took place with her father years ago. Both moments link male arousal to female helplessness—the breaking of her will, the repression of her past, the refusal to allow her a voice of protest, and the urge to restrain her physically. Although she has managed to repress this past experience, Gerald's growing excitement and ultimate refusal to release her triggers a spontaneous association, and in her rage Jessie ends up killing Gerald. As Poe's poem centers upon the narrator's compulsion for self-punishment, King finds a parallel in the fact that Jessie's bondage is not merely literal but also psychological and self-induced, the result of her own lack of self-esteem and lingering guilt. For the remainder of the novel, Jessie struggles against the voice of self-denigration and regret that reigns in "The Raven"; if she is to survive, to free herself from the bondage that represents her past and present situations, she must transcend the role of feminine passivity that has been imposed upon her by husband, father, and culture.

Direct references to "The Raven" are also made on two separate occasions in David Cronenberg's 1983 cinematic adaptation of Stephen King's novel *The Dead Zone*. The deliberate allusions to Poe's poem are impossible for a critic to overlook. Apparently Cronenberg's sympathy with King's art leads him to adopt many of his influences, particularly in the case of Poe. The intertextual referencing in *The Dead Zone* is employed for the same purpose in *Gerald's Game*: as a means for paralleling—and ultimately contrasting—the circumstances that confront the main protagonists in both works.

Most obviously, Poe's poem is about a lost love, Lenore, and the first-person male narrator's inability, or unwillingness, to shed his romantic melancholia. Poe's speaker subsists inside a room where he studies and nurtures his pain; his isolation is interrupted by the Raven, who appears only to increase his misery by ignoring the human command to "Leave my loneliness unbroken!—quit the bust above my door!" (39). The narrator does nothing to force the bird into leaving, and his questions about the destiny of the dead Lenore are rhetorically designed to end in the bird's negative comment "Nevermore." At the conclusion of the poem, we are to believe that the Raven has become a permanent resident of the narrator's room and soul; moreover, the latter appears to find a real measure of pleasure in the additional gloom afforded by the Raven's presence: "And my soul from out that shadow that lies floating on the floor/ Shall be lifted—nevermore!" (39).

Throughout *The Dead Zone*, Johnny Smith, the central consciousness of the book and film, finds himself in a position identical to the narrator in Poe's poem. He, too, has lost his love; his world's perimeters appear restricted by tragedy and loneliness; and for a major part of the film and novel, Smith flirts dangerously with indulging a propensity for cynicism and self-pity. At one point in the film, he even asks a student he tutors to read aloud the part of "The Raven" where the narrator "talks about will I ever see her again," indicating that Smith finds the parallelism impossible to ignore. But unlike the speaker in Poe's poem, whose human limitations torture him into asking the bird questions about the future—"Is there balm in Gilead?" (39)—John Smith's accident has given him possession of a power to see directly into people's lives: past, present, and future.

Smith's psychic powers link him directly to violence, particularly violence leading to death. Each time he enters the "Dead Zone," a realm that is centered in Smith even as it radiates from his touch, he "feels like [he is] dying inside." As in Poe's "bleak December" (37) setting for "The Raven," the stark winter environment that dominates the film's backdrop from the moment Smith resurfaces from his coma is meant to suggest the pervasive theme of death. William Beard notes that *The Dead Zone*'s "landscapes are wintry, the climate inhospitable, the environment a veritable waste land. . . . For most of the time this lifeless and hostile climate is simply the environment, an expression of both the objective bad luck which dogs the protagonist and his subjective sense that everything will work out for the worst" (177, 171). Every major scene in the film ends either in death or with a direct allusion to it. Afraid of fatally complicating the lives of others, and shortening his own life in the process, Smith tries to exist without human contact, to abandon his connections to the past and future, and to live according to the deliberate seclusion maintained by the speaker in "The Raven."

Like Poe's narrator, Johnny's curse is that he is condemned to speculation rather than action, and his separation from people and the world is at once a torment and a relief. Beard defines Johnny's plight in succinctly Poe-esque circumstances: "One way of describing Johnny's disease is as an inability to get out of the self. In Johnny's case this is particularly debilitating because . . . he cannot ameliorate his own situation, cannot affect his own life" (175).

As in *Gerald's Game*, *The Dead Zone* employs direct referencing to Poe's poem not only to suggest similarities, but also to supply a means for establishing contrast. For while Smith is continually attracted to the solipsism found in Poe's poem, his greater commitment is to the needs of others. And even while his great powers place him in intimate contact with the dead and dying, he ultimately dedicates his own life to the world of the living. At first it appears that the forces oppressing both Jessie and Johnny, like those in "The Raven," are purely external. But in all three of these texts the tone of helplessness and loss originates from within as much as from without. Poe's narrator, however, never emerges from his plight, never struggles to transcend his suffering, never rises against despair. Jessie Burlingame and John Smith, on the other hand, are saved from the fate of Poe's narrator because of a mutual commitment to a steady re-integration into life. While both Smith and Burlingame are tormented through most of their respective texts, their ultimate horror comes not from their own diseased psyches (as is the case in Poe's poem), but from healthy ones that stand in opposition to those that are less healthy.

In both fictional narrative and cinemagraphic adaptations of his work, Poe's presence haunts Stephen King's landscape. Whether used to inspire analogous plot and character situations, or employed to establish ultimate contrasts, over the past two and a half decades Poe's work has enriched and shaped King's fictional microcosm. As we have seen, the intersections between the two writers are cultural and psychological, as well as literary. Both their narrative styles are highly visual. Many critics have alluded to the way in which King's novels often appear to resemble screenplays and how easily his work is translated into film, and we will begin the next chapter exploring efforts to transpose Poe's fiction into film. We might thus suggest this as a final point of comparison between Poe and King: their art continues to fascinate us because, like the best of the Gothic tradition, it is as much composed of dream as it is reality.

Chapter 7

Celluloid Poe:
Detective *Noir* Meets Hollywood Gothic

A large mirror now stood where none had been perceptible before; and as I stepped up to it in extremity of terror, mine own image, but with features all pale and dabbled in blood, advanced to meet
me with a feeble and tottering gait. (Poe, "William Wilson" 130)

Poe's Gothic tales gain much of their effect from sensory exaggeration.
In "The Black Cat" the narrator proceeds through a world largely devoid
of sound. As he sinks lower and lower into the world, he is bothered by
such visual images as picking up the cat and cutting out its eye, discovering the shape of a cat with a rope around its neck impressed into the damp
plaster wall, the white splotch on the breast of the second cat. When he
turns to kill the cat and his wife interferes, however, he sinks his axe into
her brain and she collapses "without a groan." The next sound we hear is
the knocking on the wall to which there is the response of "a cry, at first
muffled and broken, like the sobbing of a child, and then quickly swelling into one long, loud, and continuous scream, utterly anomalous and in-
human—a howl!—a wailing shriek, half of horror and half of triumph,
such as might have arisen only out of hell" (207). In the same way the
only sounds we hear in "The Tell-Tale Heart" are the creak of the lantern's
cover, the beating of the old man's heart, and the scream emitted by victim and murderer when the killing is carried out. From there on in, the
narrative's sounds are limited to the quick beating of the old man's heart,
compared to the soft ticking of a clock wrapped in cotton inside the
narrator's head, which leads him to betray himself with a shriek.

Sight is used in "Ligeia" when, from the first description of Ligeia,
we are impressed with "the raven-black, the glossy, the luxuriant and natu-
rally-curling tresses" (82). When she dies, the narrator moves to England
and carries the Lady Rowena to her eerie bridal chamber. The creepy hang-
ings, whose shapes are echoed in the bedclothes and the furniture, dominate the room. The mysterious goings on in the death chamber, converted
from the recent bridal chamber, are seen, not heard: the color returns and
flees from the corpse's face, the footprint in the carpet appears as the mysterious intruder comes close to administer some drops into Rowena's restorative wine, and the final reincarnation of Ligeia occurs via her increased
height as well as in her flowing raven tresses. All these sensory details
come through the eye.

In "The Masque of the Red Death" the auditory and visual are both
represented. In Prospero's castle decorated for the masquerade ball: seven

interlocking chambers, each decorated in a different color, culminate in the last chamber, painted black with red trappings, dominated by a sable clock. The sound of the clock momentarily stops the merriment at the ball when it chimes the hour, reminding the participants of the passage of time and the inevitable approach of the end of life. But the arrival of the last uninvited guest, dressed in a black gown with a white face bedabbled with blood, coincides with the clock striking midnight. Prospero pursues the intruder, only to fall dead in the last chamber at the end of the midnight's chime. It is both sight and sound which combine to the ultimate effect of the final scene, which ironically culminates in the absence of both sight and sound.

Poe's detective stories, their crimes and murders concluded near the beginning of each story, are much less connected to sensory experience. The ratiocination of Dupin robs the tales of their immediacy, and Dupin's explanations to the narrator of what happened remove stress from the narrative; we already know the detective has solved the problem and restored the world. What film has done with Poe's detective story is to take it from a tale about the solution of a crime to transform it more into a straightforward narrative with its own dangers and immediacies. In short, the modern detective film often seeks to capitalize upon the Gothic elements inherent in its plot, characterization, and setting.

Modern film adaptations of Poe's tales have likewise highlighted their Gothic qualities, both because of the greater number of Poe tales that feature Gothic elements as well as the ease with which they can be translated from one medium to the other. Film depends on the visual and the aural, on the details of surface action. The translation of Poe's tales into film has tended to stress the same sights and sounds that Poe himself used. Hence it is interesting to note that in a film such as *The Silence of the Lambs*, which reflects the sensory emphases we have traced in Poe's Gothic tales, the sound of fluttering wings is often part of the soundtrack. Director Jonathan Demme may have decided to employ such a backdrop because of the name of the heroine, Starling, but such sounds also come to suggest the fluttering of the heart in suspenseful situations. Throughout the movie—from the fluttering of the birds as Starling completes the obstacle course under the opening credits, to the birds in the backyard of one of the murdered girls whose father Starling interviews, to the fluttering of the moths in Gumb's basement—we are never far removed from the sound.

In the early 1960s, American International Pictures produced five films based upon Poe's most popular horror tales, all directed by Roger Corman and centering upon the flamboyant persona of Vincent Price as the melancholic Poe protagonist. The AIP productions were modestly budgeted, and often this is most glaringly obvious in the employment of background settings. Shots of the same castle from the same angle, its baroque interior, and a particular section of seascape reappear in several of the films. Moreover, the majority of the films conclude with a requisite apocalyptic fire that features the aforementioned castle illuminated from flames that are superimposed from behind; indeed, each of these conflagrations employs the same footage of a burning barn or wooden rafters that has no architectural relevance whatsoever to a stone castle.

These cinematographic shortcomings notwithstanding, the Corman adaptations of Poe are true to the latter's fascination with the Gothic phantasmagoria of sensory exaggeration. Indeed, in the first of this series, *House of Usher* (1960), the film nearly overwhelms the viewer with the predominance of the color red: carpets, chairs, candles, even the doors and woodwork appear to bear a red tint. The only character associated with another color, blue, is the fiancée who escapes the final destruction. The oversaturation of red tends to operate symbolically, as it underscores the undefined and unexculpated contagion of the Usher legacy. Even the youthful Madeline, who struggles against the unhealthy atmosphere of the place, cannot escape its permutations. As Roderick (Vincent Price) acknowledges: "[The] history of the Ushers is a history of savage degradation. . . . The house itself is evil now." Corman appropriately invests his cinematographic castle with supernatural energies; the castle is a central character to the action, capable of exerting an evil influence over all who reside within. As the color red is made to permeate the interior settings of the film, casting a stain or tint over every scene, Usher's bloodline (highlighted in the quasi-incestual blood bond between Roderick and Madeline) invests the house with certain fatalism and doom.

Corman's attention to highly decorative settings, perhaps reaching the point of garish grotesque, is his most Poe-like adaptation; Corman appears to have taken seriously Poe's dictum in "The Philosophy of Composition" that the construction of any work of art "commences with the consideration of an effect" (453). From *Usher* to the last of his renditions, *The Tomb of Ligeia* (1965), Corman's emphasis on Gothic visual effects is a constant element, and actually improved in its level of sophistication as the Poe series evolved. While the burning castle is also regrettably present in the conclusion of *Ligeia*, so, too, is a real appreciation for the effects created by elaborate attention to Gothic paraphernalia, such as an ancient stone abbey in ruins and an elaborately staged dream sequence.

Of all of Corman's adaptations, *The Tomb of Ligeia* is the one that most highlights the sensual and independent potential of women. In earlier chapters we have considered Poe's perspective on fictional females—most are strong-willed, and all are beautiful, dead, or dying. Corman also shares

Poe's fascination with women; in *The Pit and the Pendulum, Masque of the Red Death*, and *The Raven*, he invents major roles for women characters not found in the original Poe narrative that contribute significantly to the development of the plot lines. Their inclusion anticipated a fundamental shift in the role of the American female, as the era of Corman's AIP films took place on the cusp of the feminist movement (Thornton 208).

Rowena occupies a role that reflects the changing status of women in the United States in the mid-sixties: she is aggressive in her courtship of Vernon, she is undaunted by his lingering obsession with the dead Ligeia, she remains determined to maintain her marriage despite being physically attacked by Vernon and the cat that embodies Ligeia's spirit. If Ligeia remains associated with the black cat that haunts this film (one of the many examples of Corman collapsing two or more Poe tales into one film), Rowena is linked to the red fox whom she is hunting when she first encounters Vernon. Ligeia bears the unpredictable traits of a feline, while Rowena is the cunning survivalist fox. In the end, Corman decides to abandon completely Poe's version of the passive pale Rowena, whose presence is merely an aid to reuniting Ligeia and the disturbed narrator. Instead, Corman's Rowena endures, not only physically, but also mentally. She is one of the few female characters in Corman's *oeuvre* (and, for that matter, all of cinema in the early 1960s) who demonstrates a level of self-reliance that defies all attempts to thwart her personality. Although these traits make her a character quite different from Poe's original Rowena, Corman's version is an ironic parallel to other independent and resilient female protagonists in Poe. She is, finally, sister to Morella and the woman who despises her most, Ligeia herself.

Roger Corman's recasting of *The Pit and the Pendulum* (1961) into a tale of mystery and madness is no surprise. The tale must be fleshed out to fill the time required of a three-reeler. What makes this film different from Poe is the responsibility of the character for his own breakdown. In Poe's stories, the characters are responsible for their own fates. The narrator of "The Black Cat" falls prey to alcoholism which leads him to the downward spiral of his life. The narrator of "The Tell-Tale Heart," in his obsession with the old man's eye and his own internal ego, strikes both at his victim and at himself. Prince Prospero of "The Masque of the Red Death" tries to deny death by shutting himself and his retinue within the walls of a castle that would keep the intruder out. While the characters possess little or no self-consciousness of their own participation in their own ruin, it comes to them with a sort of distorted justice.

Corman uses some of the same justice in the way he treats Elizabeth Medina in this film. She reenacts the unfaithfulness of Nicholas Medina's mother as well as her punishment of being buried alive. The final irony of the film is the remark by Catherine Medina that no one will ever enter the Medina torture chamber again. The camera then pans to the iron maiden that contains a tightly gagged Elizabeth, her eyes darting from side to side as she remains powerless to bring anyone's attention to her plight. Dr. Leon lies dead at the bottom of the pit with the broken mad body of Nicholas, clad in his father's hood and cape of the Inquisition.

In most of Corman's adaptations of Poe, Vincent Price plays a similar starring role. He is a figure on the edge of insanity who has inherited some familial curse that demands eventual expressions of repentance. Dignified in dress and sensorially sensitive, he dominates the action as he seems marked for some terrible fate. As is so often the case with Poe's male protagonists, premature burials haunt the Price personae. And this figure appears horrified with the possibility that he is somehow responsible for burying a lover in her crypt prematurely, as is the case in *The House of Usher*, *The Pit and the Pendulum* and *The Tomb of Ligeia*. On the other hand, the brothers and lovers that Price plays in these Corman films remain overly fascinated with the concept of premature burial to the point where the viewer must acknowledge at least a subliminal urge that motivates their actions, whether it stems from a certain ambivalence toward the women victims, a Poe-like desire for self-torment, or shaping influences from external forces. All of these motivations are at work in *The Pit and the Pendulum*.

If Poe's horror heroes/victims have the seeds of their destruction planted within their own characters, Nicholas Medina is also a victim of outside manipulation. When we first see him, he is tending to the workability of the torture devices which he has inherited along with the castle. He wants them to be in perfect working order and inspects them constantly. This may not be because of any inherent desire to torture, but because of his life-long fascination with the chamber since childhood. Nicholas had entered the dungeon as a child when his play was interrupted by his father, mother, and uncle. He hid, and witnessed the torture and death of his mother and uncle, the two guilty lovers. This pushed him toward madness, but he appears to be a rational adult, except, perhaps, for the care he gives to maintaining the condition of the instruments of torture. Such a fixation suggests that Nicholas senses a dark bond with his father's sins and the machinery used to destroy his wife and brother. And one could delve deeply into the sexual symbolism of these devices, and argue that all young men are trapped by the behavior they learn from their fathers. But Nicholas marries a wife whom he adores, even if he does not comprehend the nature of her evil. Elizabeth and Dr. Leon plan to drive him mad, and they succeed. They stage her death, her supposed premature burial, and her return to haunt Nicholas. And they succeed so well that

Nicholas's mind snaps: he turns into his father. He then reenacts the tortures on Elizabeth and Leon that his father performed on his mother Isabella and his uncle Bartolome. Nicholas's madness is less the result of his own mistakes than the manipulation of others. He is essentially an innocent, overcome by the overwhelming weight of unfortunate circumstances.

One of the last Poe adaptations that Roger Corman both directed and produced is *The Masque of the Red Death* (1964). Steven Thornton observes that it "is an ambitious film, working overtime on the metaphorical level to create an impression of high-brow cinematic legitimacy. At times it is easier to admire than to enjoy" (234). Typical to the other AIP renditions, Corman takes vast liberties with Poe's storyline: Vincent Price's Prince Prospero, in addition to being a spoiled aristocrat, is now also a Satanist; the narrative expands to include another Poe tale, "Hop-Frog," as a subplot; and Corman's version of Prospero is a libertine fascinated with personally initiating an innocent village girl named Francesca into his sordid world. This last Corman addition seems the most appropriate of all the additions; if Poe had chosen to expand "Masque," he might well have explored the perversities of Prospero's sexual appetite.

Aside from these dramatic and sometimes distracting digressions from Poe's original tale, Corman's film does a remarkable job of capturing Prospero's tyrannical and decadent nature. There is, indeed, much "that might have invited disgust" in Vincent Price's characterization. From the beginning of the film to its concluding *danse macabre*, Price's Prospero is searching for his own pleasure at the expense of others. His character is appropriately reminiscent of William Beckford's penultimate Gothic decadent, Vathek, in that Prospero quests after all manner of sensual experience—the more darkly original and entertaining the better—without fear of moral consequence and devoid of conscience. As the figure of the Red Death tells him late in the film, "Why should you be afraid to die? Your soul has been dead for a long time."

The group of party guests that Prospero has assembled with him inside the sequestered castle would be equally at home in Stephen King's Overlook Hotel, as their lusts and behavior resembling various barnyard animals confirm and reflect the direction of Prospero's spirituality. Their tightly choreographed descent into madness is one of the more engaging features of this movie. *Masque*'s elaborate costumes and large cast of secondary characters truly distinguishes this film from Corman's other works of Poe. But even more distinctive is that unlike the Poe protagonists in Corman's other films, Prospero is no long-suffering melancholic; in fact, he is the opposite of these passive recluses: an imperious personality that actively seeks to defy the human and cosmic laws of moral conduct and physical reality, as he comes to believe that he alone is immune to the ravages of the Red Death.

Detective Jake Gittes of *Chinatown* is also overwhelmed by forces larger than himself. The mysteries of Chinatown and the power of Noah Cross, appear to be too much for him. His weakness is both women—in trying to help, Gittes causes the death of one woman in his past and of Mrs. Mulwray in the present film—and justice. He wants to do more than keep the sidewalks clean, he wants to introduce order and rationality into a society which is beyond both. In many of Corman's film adaptations of Poe Tales, the Price character is destroyed by conflagration; Gittes is ruined by the incomprehensible nature of evil contained in Chinatown and only occasionally breaking out into the general society.

Chinatown, named the finest detective film of all time by the publication *The Fine Art of Murder,* is almost an archetypical detective story. (Many of the details of this film are tributes to *The Maltese Falcon,* whose director, John Huston, plays murderer Noah Cross in *Chinatown.*) The film opens with detective Gittes revealing his skills as a detective and many of the details of the detective profession. Gittes shows a client some photographs of his wife with another man, the bread and butter of the detective profession. We learn how to tell when a suspect drives away from a tryst: place a cheap watch under the wheel so that the car will smash the watch and show what time the car was moved. We see Gittes shadowing Horace Mulwray, spending long hours watching and taking photographs of Mulwray and his supposed lover. We discover how to follow a car at night: smash one of the reflectors, and it will be easier to follow the one red, one white light. We learn how to research land records in the county courthouse and, in the best hard-boiled style, how to deal with a snippy clerk.

Chinatown abounds with the core conventions of the detective story. The beautiful Mrs. Mulwray is somehow involved with the plot in ways the viewer doesn't yet understand; she inexplicably is no longer interested in finding her husband's lover. The clue to the murderer is located in a salt water garden pool, glimpsed once early by Gittes, later found to be a pair of reading glasses. We find what George Dove calls the Death Warrant when Ida Sessions, who impersonated Mrs. Mulwray at the opening of the film, calls to declare she was not responsible for the murder of Mulwray. The follow-up call, from a male caller, says that Sessions wants to see Gittes. As in the usual detective formula, Gittes will find her dead, as indeed he does. This male caller, from the police, involves Gittes even more.

The mystery is solved: Noah Cross is the murderer. He has committed the crime over the ownership of the Los Angeles water system and its future. He is connected to the murder by two clues. Mulwray was found with saltwater in his lungs despite the fact that he was found drowned in fresh water. Mulwray had a saltwater pool in his backyard. In the pool was found a pair of reading glasses that belonged to Cross. At the disclosure of these clues and the revelation of the murderer, the detective story should be over.

But it is not. There is another thread which goes against the movement of the detective story to its sense of closure. This thread is indicated by the film's title: *Chinatown*. Chinatown is where Gittes was stationed when he was a member of the police department, as was Lieutenant Escobar. There one didn't try to solve crimes but to contain them, to keep the streets clear and to make sure the laundrymen did not spit on the irons, as Gittes claims. The thread begins with Gittes repeating a joke heard in the barbershop which Mrs. Mulwray overhears, to his embarrassment. Chinese make up most of the servants in the Mulwray house while Chinatown becomes the locus of the action. Chinatown itself represents a place of confusion, the place where order breaks down. There things are never satisfactorily concluded. It is a place Gittes fears to go, but inevitably must.

While *Chinatown* contains many of the standard detective elements, it also expands beyond the conservative morality of the genre to include the forbidden topic of incest, a subject that is more of a staple to the Gothic novel than to the detective tale. Noah Cross and his daughter Evelyn were lovers for a number of years. Gittes assumes that Cross forced himself on his daughter, but both acknowledge that she was as responsible as he. From this union came Katherine, Cross's daughter and granddaughter, whom Mulwray and Mrs. Mulwray tried to protect; it is she who is the supposed lover of Mulwray. The intricate interrelationships of the characters wind up in Chinatown. Gittes has solved the crime; he should be praised in the viewer's mind. But Claude takes the glasses from Gittes and forces him to take them to Chinatown. Gittes takes them hoping that the police will be there, capture Cross, and tie up all the loose ends. But in Chinatown everything unravels as the police don't believe Gittes, Cross throws his considerable social weight around, and disaster occurs.

Here is the center of the horror that permeates Chinatown. Instead of the murderer being punished, Gittes deflects a warning shot while a policeman steps forward and kills Mrs. Mulwray. She falls on the horn, whose blasting blare is the only sound we hear. Cross comes to the side of the car, covers Katherine's eyes, and draws her into his arms, crying protective words. The film ends with a morally compromised heroine dead, her father-lover triumphantly drawing his daughter-granddaughter into his arms, and Gittes being released on the condition that he say nothing. The cops want to keep the sidewalks clear, to keep the people moving; as long as these conditions are met, everything else can be tolerated.

The detective story is about control. Poe established the principle that

Dupin's mind is strong enough to overcome the problem set forth and come to rest in a final conclusion. The horror story comes to rest in a kind of exhaustion, a struggle not to conclude definitively, but to attain a condition of stasis among its various conflicting forces. The detective story is clear, as when Sherlock Holmes establishes the conclusion of *The Hound of the Baskervilles*, in which all the evil is attributed to Stapleton. Evil is overcome, rationality reestablished. What the director, Roman Polanski, has done is to create a world too excessively burdened for the morality of the detective story; eventually *Chinatown* slides into the maelstrom of horror.

Chinatown begins as a classic detective tale, and ends in the realm of horror art. In contemporary film and popular literature, the interrelationship of detection and horror frequently takes the viewer/reader into regions that problematize the strict moral definitions that typically define the detective genre. These narratives, *Kiss the Girls, Manhunter, Tightrope, Blade Runner*, and *L·A. Confidential*, to name only a few examples, defy easy genre categorization; because of their strong reliance upon horror elements, critics tend to refer to them as *film noir*. In each of these movies it is often difficult to separate the detective from the criminal; in fact, that confusion is sometimes the central element of the plot. Harsher and bleaker than the typical detective tale, these films rely heavily upon brutality, hard-edged action, and staccato plot complications. They present an unflinching view of the American Dream's failure, at dreams that are abruptly transformed into nightmares, at lives too impoverished to dream, and the dark journeys these lives undertake. The world-weary detective in *film noir* journeys inward, saddled with his own "heart of darkness" in an urban landscape that mirrors and feeds this sense of despair. The corrupt atmospheres of these films tend to obscure moral direction and pose complicated problems that are not neatly resolved by the detective. Indeed, it is frequently the detective who turns out to be the monster at the heart of the problem.

David Fincher's film *Seven* highlights the close relationship between detective and criminal that affirms a direct line of descent linking Poe to *film noir*. In *Seven*, however, the intimacy forged between policeman and criminality is not maintained throughout the film, nor is it used to help the detective (as in Poe) capture the murderer; it is established only in the surprise conclusion. Moreover, in Poe's detective stories and typically throughout the genre, the detective ends up outwitting the criminal in solving the case. *Seven* poses a uniquely oppositional view: the detective solves the case by being outwitted by the criminal.

Inspector David Mills is a young detective recently assigned to a large urban police force. He arrives believing that he can "do some good" for humankind by arresting the forces of evil that currently engulf the city. As an older, more seasoned policeman, William Somerset has viewed the horrors that have plagued the city for too many years, to the point where he no longer "understands this place," particularly its random levels of depravity and violence. He possesses an unromantic and cynical perspective that is meant to contrast Mills's optimistic vision. As Somerset warns him, "You want to be a hero. A champion. You cannot afford to be this naive." The psychotic criminal who brings these two cops together, John Doe, embodies both these positions. Like Mills, Doe is in possession of a vision to improve mankind despite the graphic evidence of our fallen nature. Both Doe and Detective Mills believe it is their duty to foment social change; their parallel quests occur because of sin's proliferation. Mills trusts that "catching the murderers and rapists" will make the world a better place.

As Somerset and Mills both discover early on, Doe's murders are sermons to mankind. Like Hieronymus Bosch's painting "The Garden of Earthly Delights," Doe sees his mission as the enlightenment and moral edification of society through an artistic rendering of sins that are condoned and embraced on a daily basis. His work is essentially religious in nature; like some medieval prophet, his hope is to reawaken an apathetic world by employing the seven deadly sins as a teaching tool: "Wanting people to listen, you just can't tap them on the shoulder anymore. You must hit them with a sledgehammer. Then you know you've got their strict attention."

While Doe shares Mills's faith in possibilities of moral amelioration, he also embodies Somerset's disgust and anguish at the current state of social man. The same forces that have pushed Somerset to pursue early retirement have motivated John Doe to create his moralistic "masterpiece," a piece of performance art that is really a didactic treatise on evil. John Doe shares with Somerset an appreciation of the universal depravity of human nature. He understands that there are no "innocent" people, including himself; his victims have been selected because they have also been victimizers.

Mills, in contrast, simply fails to fathom the enormity and pervasiveness of sin. He does not comprehend the Gothic maxim that mankind itself is corrupt, and that everyday crime is not merely an isolated blemish on the human soul; rather, it is embedded in the very fabric of what it means to be human. His inability to understand the nature of crime and of Somerset's desire to retire from the detective's struggle with it is illustrated as the two men argue in a bar before the film's final sequence. Somerset suggests that "apathy is a solution." When Mills disagrees, Somerset asserts that Mills "wants to be a hero. You can't afford to be this naive." Mills counters by arguing that he simply doesn't want to accept the reality of evil, either through personal apathy or through inoculation. Mills concludes that, unlike Somerset, "I care."

Doe appears to sense that Mills must learn the truth about evil for himself, so he makes the detective into an unwitting student. After Mills has entered his ghastly apartment, Doe tells him on the telephone that he "admires" him. Later, Doe assigns the sin of envy to himself because Mills lives the life of a simple man in possession of a beautiful and pure wife. But Doe's envy may also include Mills's ability to walk blindly through the world of sin—to not collapse under the knowledge of its presence and self-destructive potential. Mills's existence is easier and less painful than what Doe and Somerset experience because the young policeman remains deliberately insulated from evil's reality. This innocent ignorance creates a bizarre level of envy in Doe; it is why he chooses Mills as the audience to be initiated into the world of despair and corruption.

By clinging to his naive faith in the power of his own righteous goodness, Mills also fails to see clearly the essential limitations of his own nature. Somerset warns him throughout the film that he must remain in control of his emotions, particularly his propensity toward anger. But on each occasion, Mills betrays himself, from the incident with Doe posing as a photographer on the stairs to his final choice at the end of the film to "become Wrath." In photographing Mills, just as he has photographed his other victim-participants, John Doe uncovers the potential Wrath that Mills barely manages to restrain. The detective must learn the lesson of his own corruption, as Doe predicts, "every time [Mills] looks in the mirror."

It is the monster who confronts the most complex and demanding issues, who is the tragic stimulus, who kills and tortures, and is, in turn, killed and tortured himself. It is also the monster who, by virtue of his otherness, possesses the potential to teach us something fundamental about ourselves and our humanity. In *Seven*, Doe's morality play has forced Mills into direct contact with what he has passionately denied: his own intimate connection to evil and the capacity to sin. John Doe is representative of everything Mills has repressed in himself. This is why their conversation in the car on the way to the film's climax is so contentious: Doe emerges from the underside of the city, he is Mills's dark brother of violence, ascending from the subconscious to confront the detective directly and demand acknowledgment. Even as Mills rebuffs every attempt by Doe to establish their kinship, it is clear that Doe is right to argue that the two men share an inextricable bond in their mutual attraction to violence, in their passionate desire to perform moral action, in Doe's choice to "play husband" with Tracy Mills, and in the culmination of Doe's morality play.

In addition to his propensity toward violent displays of anger, Mills's youthful career zealotry blinds him to the emotional needs of his young wife, Tracy. He uproots her from a satisfying life and teaching career to bring her to the city, a place that she obviously hates. But rather than focus attention on her adjustment, he tries to pacify her with empty assurances that "she'll get used to it." Mills actually demonstrates more affection toward his dogs, whom he calls his children, than he does to his wife. Is it any wonder, then, that Tracy Mills shares the news of her pregnancy with Somerset, who is virtually a stranger, before she tells her husband?

Tracy Mills understands that her husband would view her pregnancy with the same simple-minded attitude he has on crime. As she contemplates aborting the child because the city appears to be such a terrible place to raise it, she turns to Somerset for guidance. Unlike her husband, his perspective is broader, more capable of incorporating her concerns in bringing a child into a world so corrupt and cruel. Somerset has long immersed himself in the complexity of moral issues that have likewise obsessed John Doe, and thus he is in a position to address Tracy's darkest fears.

Only at the end of the film, when Somerset decides to delay his retirement to capture Doe and then assures the police chief with the words, "I'll be around," do we recognize that the drama that has come to center on Mills and John Doe has somehow also affected Somerset. The Doe case has certainly reawakened Somerset's passion for detective work, but it is Mills's personal sacrifice that apparently recharges Somerset's commitment to his fellow man. In fact, one might argue that Doe forces Mills and Somerset to exchange philosophical orientations at the end of *Seven*. "If you shoot him," Somerset warns Mills unsuccessfully, "[Doe] will win," because he will have succeeded in erasing the line that separates the monster from the human. Although on this occasion Somerset fails to convince Mills of its importance, the fact that he argues the position at this crucial point in the film underscores Somerset's commitment to it. This commitment is echoed in the voice-over at the end of the film, when Somerset says: "Ernest Hemingway once wrote, 'The world is a fine place and worth fighting for.' I agree with the second part." Somerset, as the experienced detective, sees into the depths of evil in this world and acknowledges the world's meanness. More mature than Mills, he knows that, evil or not, the world is worth fighting for. Overly optimistic or not, it is the creed of the detective.

One of the more interesting aspects of this film is the fact that it problematizes easy distinctions between criminal and detective. In this way, *Seven* closely resembles narratives such as *Chinatown, Tightrope, Blade Runner*, and *Manhunter*: all of these films come to blur the separation of criminal and police. The conclusion of *Seven* restores superficial order and control over the chaos that has been unleashed upon the city: Doe is dead, his serial quest is over, and Somerset appears to be reconsidering keeping his job with the police force a while longer. But Doe has also succeeded in his goal to make his "masterpiece" extend beyond the limits of his own life. In making the choice to become Wrath to avenge his wife's death, Mills also becomes a monster who murders an unarmed suspect. In becoming the last of Doe's victims, Mills's optimistic faith is shattered; he has lost not only his beautiful wife, but also his career, his freedom, and his sanity.

Consequently, the viewer of this film does not share in the sense of security traditionally associated with the detective genre's apprehension and abatement of criminal behavior. *Seven* remains a bleak and relentless Gothic journey into the darkest regions of the human psyche. Set in a rain-stained urban landscape that features brilliant camera work that frequently descends into the bowels of the city's underworld, the only time we emerge from this Poe-like claustrophobia is at its conclusion, which takes place in open terrain. But even here, the brooding darkness of the film is barely lightened. John Doe's capture necessitates further police work; the criminal remains in control even after he is placed under arrest. His insistence that Mills and Somerset continue to participate in his metatextual drama ends up subverting the easy definitions that Mills and the viewer employ to distinguish good from evil, ethical enthusiast from monstrous criminal.

In addition to highlighting the interconnection between horror and detection that has been a primary consideration throughout this book, *Seven* is a film, as we have seen, that problematizes the epistemology of the monster. We understand that John Doe's actions are monstrous throughout, but it is only in this film's startling conclusion that we are forced to accommodate a more inclusive definition of monstrosity. If the good man, a well-intentioned policeman, can be destroyed so completely, what hope do any of us have against the power of corruption? It is possible to posit that the darker the detective tale—that is, the more ambiguous the role, behavior, or philosophical orientation of the individual detective in it— the more difficult it becomes to distinguish detection from Gothic horror.

Perhaps Ridley Scott's 1982 futuristic narrative, *Blade Runner*, makes this point more convincingly than any other recent film or novel. Set in a rain-soaked urban world that very closely resembles that of *Seven*, *Blade Runner* likewise blurs not only the roles of policeman (blade runner) and monster (replicant), but the very perimeters of *genre* itself, as the film is at once a *film noir* detective adventure, a science-fiction fantasy, a dystopian critique, a Christian allegory, and a monster tale. But most interesting to the purposes of this book, *Blade Runner* is also a narrative of doublings, of Poe-esque mirrorings and mergings of good and evil to the point where these polarities eventually collapse into one another and lose their clarification. (Perhaps this is a possible explanation for the film's lack of commercial success, while it has attained enormous scholarly attention. By 1990, there were over 300 analyses of *Blade Runner*, including books and journal articles [Rushing and Frentz 143].) Even the title itself suggests doublings, as a blade has two sides to it and cuts objects into halves, while the concept of a runner in this film is also divisible, as the narrative questions continually who is running from whom?

The theme of the double or secreted self occurs in several Poe stories. Surely the means by which Dupin comes to identify with the criminal psyche implies a certain level of doubling, and even the close interaction and identification between murderer and victim in tales such as "The Tell-Tale Heart" and "The Cask of Amontillado" complicates the act of criminality. Poe's use of the double theme, however, is given its most explicit expression in "William Wilson." The narrator recalls the annoying presence in his life of a figure that is identical in bodily appearance, but the narrator's moral and intellectual opposite. The story is an attempt not only to contrast the behavior of these two figures, but likewise to show their interdependency. This same struggle for recognition of opposing forces is at work in *Blade Runner*, a film that highlights the conflict between monster and human at the same time as it strives to illustrate their greater points of convergence.

In all of Poe's tales in which the theme of the double predominates, issues of repression, shadowed selves, and sublimation are central to any interpretation. The demise of the old man in "The Tell-Tale Heart," for example, prefigures the eventual self-destruction of his murderer; in Poe, as we have traced elsewhere, victim and victimizer become one and the same. *Blade Runner* parallels Poe insofar as it is a film that likewise complicates, and eventually negates, distinctions between "good man" and monster, hunter and prey, human and other. As J. P. Telotte argues, "This indistinguishability, a nearly perfect nemesis, gives birth to the film's central conflict, as the replicants threaten to render their creators superfluous and take their place" (154–55).

Rick Deckard, the detective who is the blade runner in charge of eliminating replicants who rebel against their status as machines "more human than human," gradually learns that he has more in common with his prey than he does with the technobureaucracy that seeks to control them both. Designed with artificial four-year life spans that apparently are genetically encoded to maintain optimum control, the androids in *Blade Runner* return to earth seeking greater longevity. With their lethal superior strength and intelligence, the replicants evoke fear in humans, and any attempt to infiltrate human society is deemed a criminal offense, punishable by death from blade runners, a division of the police who are authorized to destroy rebel machines. (Their banishment also clearly reflects the human fear of being displaced by superior beings.) However, each time Deckard "terminates" one of the renegade replicants, he is forced into a greater and more intimate appreciation of their suffering and precarious situation. As his voice-over betrays after the killing of Zhora: "Replicants weren't supposed to have feelings. Neither were blade runners. What the hell was happening to me?" In fact, on each of these occasions Deckard puts himself in a position where his own life is threatened; although he manages to kill the replicants, he barely avoids getting killed himself. In the acts of hunting and performing violence, Deckard, in turn, is hunted and threatened himself.

All of this is to suggest that Deckard's participation in this gruesome police work represents a learning process. As in Poe, the act of perpetrating violence begets violence, against the self and one's most essential sense of humanity. Throughout the film and in Philip K. Dick's novel upon which the movie was based, Deckard's identity as a possible replicant is frequently questioned. Whether in reality he is or is not an android seems a moot point in light of the fact that Deckard is forced into a position where he must experience life from the unique perspective of a replicant—especially in terms of repressing his feelings and avoiding violent death. As Roy Batty, the leader of the replicants, acknowledges, "Quite an experience to live in fear, isn't it? That's what it is like to be a slave." As the most intelligent of the rebel cyborgs, Roy comes to recognize the metonymic bond between human and other on a level that no one else in the film quite comprehends, including Deckard himself. This shared bond is the main reason Roy allows Deckard to live, in fact, saves his life by catching the policeman as he falls off the roof and pulls him up to safety. Deckard is only partially right when he speculates that "Maybe in those last moments [Roy] loved life more than he ever had before." A more compelling justification is that Roy is profoundly aware of his role as Deckard's teacher and double. He has observed all of Deckard's actions in the course of the narrative, and at the end is aware that Batty's suffering, loss, and close proximity to death have been simultaneously mirrored in the blade runner's own experience. Like Deckard, Batty struggles with his conscience: "I've done questionable things," he confesses to his creator, Tyrell. But where Deckard continually represses his feelings about murdering as a "part of the business," Batty changes in the course of the film from prodigal son-warrior to reflective poet.

Unlike John Doe, who provides Detective Mills with a dramatic initiation into evil and personal corruption, Roy's lesson for Deckard is one of spiritual redemption. Thus, while both *Seven* and *Blade Runner* are narratives where the detectives intersect with their ferocious nemeses, this intimate contact produces decidedly contrasting results. As we have seen, Mills loses his humanity in becoming the raging monster; Deckard, on the other hand, appears to find his by drawing Roy's animus spirit into his own soul.

As in the traditional *film noir*, the detective discovers something other than what he was hired to investigate, and this is often a moral response to abuses of power in civilization (Rushing and Frentz 156). Batty's last speech is perhaps the most poignant plea for the sanctity of life uttered since Mary Shelley's monster made a similar argument two centuries earlier. His last words signify the fragility of existence and an acceptance of its impermanence, "lost in time, like tears in rain." While Dr. Frankenstein chooses to remain impervious to his creature's lament, Deckard finally comes to embrace his shadow double—the monstrous other—and the two become one. As Joseph Francavilla has noted in his discussion of literary and mythological doubles, "The intimate, unbreakable bond between doubles indicates an empathic, love-hate relationship whose development goes well beyond mere coincidence or chance. Significantly, the death of one self almost always implies the death of some important aspect of the other self" (5). Roy's choice to save Deckard completes the transference of the replicant's spirit, symbolized in the released dove, to the blade runner. Monster becomes human in this unselfish act; and human, in turn, learns that by denying the humanity of the other, he has behaved monstrously. Francavilla observes that "in saving Deckard, Batty understands he is saving until the last minute that part of himself which is truly human" (11). But Roy's actions are motivated by more than just an urge for self-perpetuation. In death Roy gives meaning to *Deckard's* life, as is revealed in *Blade Runner's* final scene: Deckard returns to his apartment to deliver to Rachel, another replicant, the same gift of acceptance and redemption that Roy has just conferred upon the detective.

The films discussed in this chapter can be viewed as both expressions of the detective and horror genres and expansions beyond their critically accepted perimeters. Both of us believe that if Poe were alive today, he might be involved in the film industry, using this medium as a vehicle for expressing the same psychological torments and visual effects found in his literary narratives. As any careful reader of Poe will immediately recognize, the writer frequently employed large tapestries and curtains painted with grotesque portraits deliberately animated to create a moving visual image. In "Ligeia," for example, the walls of Rowena's bridal chamber are covered with ghastly "arabesque figures" painted upon floor-to-ceiling tapestries "vastly heightened by the artificial introduction of a strong continual current of wind behind the draperies—giving a hideous and uneasy animation to the whole" (89). Although published more than half a century before the advent of motion pictures, Poe's description of this scene suggests nothing less than a cinemagraphic image.

For that matter, Poe's entire phantasmagoric *oeuvre* is ideally suited for larger-than-life projection and the surreal possibilities of film. Indeed, when Poe asserts in "The Philosophy of Composition" that the ultimate purpose of art is to "produce continuously novel effects" (457), he could just as easily be describing the goal of a contemporary Hollywood director or producer, such as Roger Corman, as he has assumed the role of the poet. His decision to reveal the creative process that resulted in the production of "The Raven," to "let the public take a peep behind the scenes" (454), is really the nineteenth-century equivalent of *Hearts of Darkness* (a film about the production of the film *Apocalypse Now*) or *The Making of Titanic*: a metatextual document about the composing process of a tremendously popular work of art.

Works Cited

Aliens. Dir. Ridley Scott. Brandywine Productions, 1979.

Auden, W. H. "The Guilty Vicarage." *The Dyer's Hand*. New York: Random House, 1988.

Beard, William. "An Anatomy of Melancholy: Cronenberg's *Dead Zone*." *Journal of Canadian Studies* 27 (1992–93): 169–79.

Beckford, William. *Vathek*. 1786. New York: Dutton, 1967.

Bellamy, Joe David. "The Dark Lady of American Letters: An Interview with Joyce Carol Oates." *Atlantic* February 1972: 63–67.

Blade Runner. Dir. Ridley Scott. Blade Runner Partnership/Ladd Co., 1982.

The Blob. Dir. Irwin S. Yeaworth, Jr. Tonylyn Production, 1958.

Bonaparte, Marie. *The Life and Works of Edgar Allan Poe: A Psychoanalytic Interpretation*. Trans. John Rodker. London: Hogarth Press, 1949.

Borgo, Susan. *Unbearable Weight: Feminism, Western Culture, and the Body*. Berkeley: U of California P, 1993.

Caputi, Jane. *The Age of Sex Crimes*. Bowling Green, OH: Bowling Green State University Popular Press, 1987.

Carroll, Noël. *The Philosophy of Horror, or Paradoxes of the Heart*. New York: Routledge, 1990.

Chandler, Raymond. *The Big Sleep*. New York: Vintage, 1976.

Chinatown. Dir. Roman Polanski. Paramount, 1974.

Christie, Agatha. *The Murder of Roger Ackroyd*. New York: Pocket Books, 1954.

Clover, Carol. *Men, Women, and Chain Saws: Gender in the Modern Horror Film*. Princeton: Princeton UP, 1992.

Crane, Jonathan Lake. *Terror and Everyday Life: Singular Moments in the History of the Horror Film*. Thousand Oaks, CA: Sage, 1994.

Creighton, Joanne V. *Joyce Carol Oates: Novels of the Middle Years*. New York: Twayne, 1992.

"Dark Victory." *The Nation* 20 April 1992: 507–8.

Davidson, Edward H., ed. *Selected Writings of Edgar Allan Poe*. Boston: Houghton Mifflin Company, 1956.

Dayan, Joan. "Amorous Bondage: Poe, Ladies, and Slaves." *The American Face of Edgar Allan Poe*. Eds. Shawn Rosenheim and Stephen Rachman. Baltimore: Johns Hopkins UP, 1995. 179–209.

Dead Zone, The. Dir. David Cronenberg. Dino De Laurnetiis/Lorimar, 1983.

Dick, Philip K. *Do Androids Dream of Electric Sheep?* New York: Ballantine, 1968.

Dickerson, Mary Jane. "Stephen King Reading William Faulkner: Memory, Desire, and Time in the Making of *IT*." *The Dark Descent: Essays Defining Stephen King's Horrorscape*. Ed. Tony Magistrale. Westport, CT: Greenwood Press, 1992. 171–86.

Dostoevsky, Fyodor. *Crime and Punishment*. 1866. Trans. David Magarshack. Baltimore, MD: Penguin, 1951.

———. *Notes from Underground*. 1864. Trans. Andrew R. MacAndrew. New York: New American Library, 1961.

Dove, George N. *The Reader and the Detective Story*. Bowling Green, OH: Bowling Green State University Popular Press, 1997.

Doyle, Arthur Conan. "The Adventure of the Final Problem." *The Original Illustrated Sherlock Holmes*. Secaucus, NJ: Castle, n.d. 327–39.

———. *The Hound of the Baskervilles*. 1902. *The Original Illustrated Sherlock Holmes*. Secaucus, NJ: Castle, n.d. 341–445.

———. "A Scandal in Bohemia." 1891. *The Original Illustrated Sherlock Holmes*. Secaucus, NJ: Castle, n.d. 11–25.

———. *A Study in Scarlet*. 1887. New York: Penguin, 1985.

Edmundson, Mark. *Nightmare on Main Street: Angels, Sadomasochism, and the Culture of the Gothic*. Cambridge, MA: Harvard UP, 1997.

Eliot, T. S. "From Poe to Valery." *Hudson Review* 2 (1949): 327–42.

Elmer, Jonathan. *Reading at the Social Limit: Affect, Mass Culture and Edgar Allan Poe*. Stanford: Stanford UP, 1995.

Evans, Walter. "Movie Monsters: A Sexual Theory." *Common Culture: Reading and Writing about American Popular Culture*. Eds. Michael Petracca and Madeleine Sorapure. Upper Saddle River, NJ: Prentice-Hall, 1998. 501–9.

Fiedler, Leslie A. *Waiting for the End*. New York: Dell, 1964.

Fisher, Benjamin Franklin. "The Residual Gothic Impulse: 1824–1873." *Horror Literature*. Ed. Marshall B. Tymn. New York: Bowker Company, 1981. 176–89.

Fowler, Christopher. "The Master Builder." *The Bureau of Lost Souls*. New York: Ballantine, 1989. 161–93.

Francavilla, Joseph. "The Android as *Doppelgänger*." *Retrofitting Blade Runner*. Ed. Judith B. Kerman. Bowling Green, OH: Bowling Green University Popular Press, 1991. 4–15.

Frank, Frederick, S. "The Gothic Romance: 1762–1820." *Horror Literature*. Ed. Marshall B. Tymn. New York: Bowker Company, 1981. 3–33.

Friday the 13th. Dir. Sean S. Cunningham. Georgetown Productions, Paramount, 1980.

Fuss, Diana. *Identification Papers*. New York: Routledge, 1995.

Garrett, Greg. "Objecting to Objectification: Reviewing the Feminine in *The Silence of the Lambs*." *Journal of Popular Culture* 27 (1994): 1–12.

Gorman, Ed, et al., eds. *The Fine Art of Murder: The Mystery Reader's Indispensible Companion*. New York: Carroll & Graf, 1993.

Grafton, Sue. *"A" Is for Alibi*. New York: Holt, Rinehart, and Winston, 1982.

———. *"G" Is for Gumshoe*. New York: Fawcett Crest, 1991.

———. *"I" Is for Innocent*. New York: Henry Holt and Company, 1992.

———. *"J" Is for Judgment*. Henry Holt and Company, 1993.

Graham, Judith, ed. *Current Biography Yearbook, 1994*. New York: H. W. Wilson, 1994.

Grimes, Martha. *The Five Bells and Bladebone*. Boston: Little Brown and Company, 1987.

Haas, Lynda, and Robert Haas. "Living with(out) Boundaries: The Novels of Anne Rice." *A Dark Night's Dreaming: Contemporary American Horror Fiction*. Eds. Tony Magistrale and Michael Morrison. Columbia: South Carolina UP, 1996. 55–67.

Halberstam, Judith. *Skin Shows: Gothic Horror and the Technology of Monsters*. Durham, NC: Duke UP, 1995.

Halloween. Dir. John Carpenter. Falcon Films, 1978.

Hammett, Dashiell. "The Golden Horseshoe." *The Continental Op*. New York: Random House, 1974. 43–90.

———. *The Maltese Falcon*. 1929. New York: Vintage, 1972.

Harris, Thomas. *Black Sunday*. New York: New American Library, 1975.

———. *Red Dragon*. New York: Penguin, 1981.

———. *The Silence of the Lambs*. New York: St. Martin's, 1988.

Hawthorne, Nathaniel. "The Birthmark." *The Complete Novels and Selected Tales of Nathaniel Hawthorne*. New York: The Modern Library, 1937. 1021–33.

Haycraft, Howard. *The Art of the Mystery Story*. New York: Carroll & Graf, 1983.

———. *Murder for Pleasure*. New York: Carroll & Graf, 1984.

Hearts of Darkness. Dir. Fax Bahr, Eleanor Coppola. Showtime Network, 1991.

House of Usher. Dir. Roger Corman. American International Pictures, 1960.

Housewright, David. *Penance*. New York: Foul Play Books, 1995.

"Judge Lynch." "Battle of the Sexes: The Judge and His Wife Look at Mysteries." *The Art of the Mystery Story*. Ed. Howard Haycraft. New York: Carroll & Graf, 1983. 367–72.

Keating, H. R. F. *Crime and Mystery: The One Hundred Best Books*. New York: Carroll & Graf, 1988.

Kent, Brian. "Stephen King and His Readers: A Dirty, Compelling Romance." *A Casebook on the Stand*. Ed. Anthony Magistrale. Mercer Island, WA: Starmont House, 1992. 37–68.

King, Stephen. *Apt Pupil*. *Different Seasons*. New York: Viking, 1982.

———. *The Body*. *Different Seasons*. New York: Viking, 1982.

———. *Carrie*. New York: Doubleday, 1976.

———. *Danse Macabre*. New York: Berkley Books, 1982.

———. *The Dark Half*. New York: Viking, 1989.

———. *The Dead Zone*. New York: Viking, 1979.

———. "Dolan's Cadillac." *Nightmares and Dreamscapes*. New York: Viking, 1993. 11–66.

———. *Dolores Claiborne*. New York: Viking, 1993.

———. *Gerald's Game*. New York: Viking, 1992.

———. *IT*. New York: Viking, 1986.

———. *Needful Things*. New York: Viking, 1991.

———. *Pet Sematary*. New York: Doubleday, 1983.

———. *Rose Madder*. New York: Viking, 1995.

136

———. *The Shawshank Redemption. Different Seasons*. New York: Viking, 1982.

———. *The Shining*. New York: Viking, 1977.

———. *The Stand*. New York: Doubleday, 1990.

———. "Why We Crave Horror Movies." *Common Culture: Reading and Writing about American Popular Culture*. Eds. Michael Petracca and Madeleine Sorapure. Upper Saddle River, NJ: Prentice Hall, 1998. 498–500.

Kiss the Girls. Dir. Gary Fleder. Rysher Entertainment, Paramount, 1997.

Klein, Kathleen Gregory. *The Woman Detective: Gender and Genre*. Urbana: Illinois UP, 1995.

L. A. Confidential. Dir. Curtis Hanson. Warner Bros., 1997.

Lawrence, D. H. *Studies in Classical American Literature*. New York: Penguin, 1925.

Leverenz, David. "Poe and Gentry Virginia." *The American Face of Edgar Allan Poe*. Eds. Shawn Rosenheim and Stephen Rachman. Baltimore: Johns Hopkins UP, 1995. 10–36.

Lewis, Matthew G. *The Monk*. 1795. New York: Grove, 1952.

Lovecraft, H. P. *Supernatural Horror in Literature*. New York: Dover, 1973.

Magistrale, Tony. "Hawthorne's Woods Revisited: Stephen King's *Pet Sematary*." *Nathaniel Hawthorne Review* 14 (1988): 9–13.

Manhunter. Dir. Michael Mann. Anchor Bay Entertainment, 1986.

Manlove, Colin N. "'Closer Than an Eye': The Interconnections of Stevenson's *Dr. Jekyll and Mr. Hyde*." *The Dark Fantastic: Selected Essays from the Ninth International Conference on the Fantastic in the Arts*. Ed. C.W. Sullivan III. Westport, CT: Greenwood Press, 1997. 3–13.

Masque of the Red Death. Dir. Roger Corman. American International Pictures, 1964.

Masse, Michele A. *In the Name of Love: Women, Masochism, and the Gothic*. Ithaca, NY: Cornell UP, 1992.

Mathiessen, F. O. *American Renaissance*. New York: Oxford UP, 1941.

Milazzo, Lee, ed. *Conversations with Joyce Carol Oates*. Jackson: Mississippi UP, 1989.

Morgan, Robin. *The Demon Lover: On the Sexuality of Terrorism*. New York: Norton, 1989.

Mustazza, Leonard. "The Red Death's Sway: Setting and Character in Poe's 'The Masque of the Red Death' and King's *The Shining*." *The Shining Reader*. Ed. Anthony Magistrale. Mercer Island, WA: Starmont House, 1991. 105–20.

Nabokov, Vladimir. "Introduction." *The Strange Case of Dr. Jekyll and Mr. Hyde*. New York: Signet, 1987. 7–34.

Nietzsche, Friedrich. "Dionysos and Apollo." Eds. Richard Ellmann and Charles Feidelson, Jr. *The Modern Tradition: Backgrounds of Modern Literature*. New York: Oxford UP, 1965. 548–58.

Nightmare on Elm Street, A. Dir. Wes Craven. New Line Cinema, 1984.

Oates, Joyce Carol. "Bloodstains." *Night-Side*. New York: Vanguard Press, 1977. 168–85.

———. "The Dungeon." *Night-Side*. New York: Vanguard Press, 1977. 134–48.

———. "The Premonition." *Haunted: Tales of the Grotesque*. New York: Dutton, 1994. 172–87.

———. "Where Are You Going, Where Have You Been?" *Selected Early Stories of Joyce Carol Oates*. New York: Ontario Review Press, 1993. 118–36.

———. "The White Cat." *Haunted: Tales of the Grotesque*. New York: Dutton, 1994. 72–96.

Panek, Leroy Lad. *An Introduction to the Detective Story*. Bowling Green, OH: Bowling Green State University Popular Press, 1987.

——. *Watteau's Shepherds: The Detective Novel in Britain: 1914–1940*. Bowling Green, OH: Bowling Green State University Popular Press, 1979.

Paretsky, Sara. *Bitter Medicine*. New York: Ballantine Books, 1988.

——. "Soft Spot for Serial Murderers." *New York Times* 28 April 1991, natl. ed.: sec. 4, 17.

Paul, Robert S. *Whatever Happened to Sherlock Holmes: Detective Fiction, Popular Theology and Society*. Carbondale: Southern Illinois UP, 1991.

The Pit and the Pendulum. Dir. Roger Corman. American International Pictures, 1961.

Poe, Edgar Allan. "The Balloon Hoax." 1844. *Complete Stories and Poems of Edgar Allan Poe*. New York: Doubleday, n.d. 496–505.

——. *Complete Stories and Poems of Edgar Allan Poe*. 1844. New York: Doubleday, n. d.

——. "Descent into the Maelstrom." 1841. *Complete*. 108–20.

——. "Eleonora." 1845. Poe, *Complete* 513–17.

——. "Morella." 1835. Poe, *Complete* 222–26.

——. "The Mystery of Marie Roget." 1842–43. Poe, *Complete* 27–63.

——. "The Premature Burial." 1844. Poe, *Complete* 261–71.

——. "Thou Art the Man." 1844. Poe, *Complete* 226–36.

——. "Annabel Lee." 1849. Davidson 46–47.

——. "The Black Cat." 1843. Davidson 199–208.

——. "The Cask of Amontillado." 1846. Davidson 231–37.

——. "The Fall of the House of Usher." 1839. Davidson 95–112.

——. "Hop Frog." 1849. Davidson 237–46.

——. "The Imp of the Perverse." 1845. Davidson 225–30.

———. "Ligeia." 1838. Davidson 80–94.

———. "The Man of the Crowd." 1840. Davidson 131–39.

———. "The Mask of the Red Death." 1842. Davidson 174–80.

———. "Metzengerstein." 1832. Davidson 61–69.

———. "The Murders in the Rue Morgue." 1841. Davidson 139–71.

———. "The Philosophy of Composition." 1846. Davidson 452–63.

———. "The Pit and the Pendulum." 1843. Davidson 180–94.

———. "The Poetic Principle." 1850. Davidson 464–85.

———. "The Purloined Letter." 1844–45. Davidson 208–25.

———. "The Raven." 1845. Davidson 36–39.

———. "The Tell-Tale Heart." 1843. Davidson 194–99.

———. "Ulalume." 1847. Davidson 39–42.

———. "William Wilson." 1839. Davidson 112–30.

Poe, Edgar Allan. *Eureka: A Prose Poem.* 1848. *Collected Writings of Edgar Allan Poe.* 4 vols. Ed. Burton R. Pollin. Boston: Twayne, 1981. 185–354.

Psycho. Dir. Alfred Hitchcock. Shamley Productions, 1960.

Rajan, Gita. "A Feminist Reading of Poe's 'The Tell-Tale Heart'." *Papers on Language and Literature* 24 (1988): 283–300.

The Raven. Dir. Roger Corman. American International Pictures, 1963.

Rear Window. Dir. Alfred Hitchcock. Paramount, 1954.

Reesman, Jeanne Campbell. "Riddle Games: Stephen King's Metafictive Dialogue." *The Dark Descent: Essays Defining Stephen King's Horrorscape.* Ed. Tony Magistrale. Westport, CT: Greenwood Press, 1992. 157–70.

Ross, Alex. "Most Wanted." *The New Yorker* 11 August 1997: 76–79.

Rushing, Janice Hocker, and Thomas S. Frentz. *Projecting the Shadow: The Cyborg Hero in American Film*. Chicago: Chicago UP, 1995.

Sayers, Dorothy L. *Gaudy Night*. New York: Avon, 1968.

Schaffer, Rachel. "Armed (With Wit) & Dangerous: Sue Grafton's Sense of Black Humor." *The Armchair Detective* 30 (1997): 316–22.

Seven. Dir. David Fincher. New Line Cinema, 1995.

Shakespeare, William. *Hamlet*. 1603–4. New York: Oxford UP, 1987.

———. *The Tempest*. 1623. New York: Oxford UP, 1987.

Shelley, Mary. *Frankenstein. Frankenstein, Dracula,* and *Dr. Jekyll and Mr. Hyde*. New York: Signet, 1978.

Sheridan, Daniel. "Later Victorian Ghost Stories: The Literature of Belief." *Gothic* 2.2 (1980): 33–39.

Shining, The. Dir. Stanley Kubrick. Warner Bros./Peregrine Hawk Films, 1980.

The Silence of the Lambs. Dir. Jonathan Demme. Orion Pictures, 1991.

Simmons, Dan. "Shapeshifters and Skinwalkers: The Writer's Curse of Negative Capability." *Journal of the Fantastic in the Arts* 8.4 (1997): 398–418.

Skal, David. "The Monster That Devoured Publishing." *Gadfly* 1.8 (October 1997): 17.

Sophocles. *Oedipus Rex*. Trans. Dudley Fitts and Robert Fitzgerald. *Angles of Vision*. Eds. Arthur W. Biddle and Toby Fulwiler. New York: MacGraw Hill, 1992. 767–809.

Soukup, Barbara. "'The Premonition' by Joyce Carol Oates." Internet version: http://www.usfca.edu/southerr/premonition.htmltac-statt/

Stasio, Marilyn. "Lady Gumshoes Boiled Less Hard." *New York Times Book Review* 28 April 1985: 1, 39–40.

Stevenson, Robert Louis. *Dr. Jekyll and Mr. Hyde*. 1886. New York: Signet, 1987.

Stoker, Bram. *Dracula.* 1897. New York: W. W. Norton, 1997.

Symons, Julian. *Bloody Murder: From the Detective Story to the Crime Novel.* 2nd ed. New York: Penguin Books, 1985.

Telotte, J. P. "The Doubles of Fantasy and the Space of Desire." *Film Criticism* 11.1–2 (fall-winter 1987): 43–55.

Tessier, Thomas. "The Big Producer." *Reign of Fear: The Fiction and Films of Stephen King.* Ed. Don Herron. Novato, CA: Underwood-Miller, 1988. 69–78.

The Texas Chain Saw Massacre. Dir. Tobe Hooper. Vortex, 1974.

Tharp, Julie. "The Transvestite Monster: Gender Horror in *The Silence of the Lambs* and *Psycho.*" *Journal of Popular Film and Television* 19 (1991): 106–13.

The Thing. Dir. John Carpenter. Universal City Studios, 1982.

Thornton, Steven. "The Women of American International Pictures." *Bitches, Bimbos, and Virgins: Women in the Horror Film.* Eds. Gary and Susan Svehla. Baltimore: Midnight Marquee Press, Inc., 1996. 207–45.

Tightrope. Dir. Richard Toggle. Warner Bros., 1984.

The Tomb of Ligeia. Dir. Roger Corman. American International Pictures, 1965.

Trott, Nancy Roberts. "Murder Suspect Just 'a Nice Guy.'" *The Burlington Free Press* 2 January 1995: 1A

Twitchell, James. *Dreadful Pleasures: An Anatomy of Modern Horror.* New York: Oxford UP, 1985.

Underwood, Tim, and Chuck Miller, eds. *Bare Bones: Conversations on Terror with Stephen King.* New York: McGraw-Hill, 1988.

Van Dine, S. S. "Twenty Rules for Writing Detective Stories." *The Art of the Mystery Story.* Ed. Howard Haycraft. New York: Carroll & Graf, 1993. 189–93.

Van Doren Stern, Philip. "Introduction." *The Portable Poe*. New York: Viking, 1946. xv–xxxviii.

Weber, Jean-Paul. "Edgar Poe or the Theme of the Clock." *Poe: A Collection of Critical Essays*. Ed. Robert Regan. Englewood Cliffs, NJ: Prentice Hall, 1967. 79–97.

Williams, Linda. "When the Woman Looks." *The Dread of Difference: Gender and the Horror Film*. Ed. Barry Keith Grant. Austin: Texas UP, 1996. 15–34.

Wilson, Edmund. "Who Cares Who Killed Roger Ackroyd?" *The Art of the Mystery Story*. Ed. Howard Haycraft. New York: Carroll & Graf, 1983. 390–97.

Winter, Douglas E. *Stephen King: The Art of Darkness*. New York: New American Library, 1984.

Wolf, Leonard, ed. *The Essential Dr. Jekyll and Mr. Hyde*. New York: Plume, 1995.

Wood, Robin. *Hitchcock's Films*. New York: Castle Books, 1969.

———. *Hollywood from Vietnam to Reagan*. New York: Columbia UP, 1986.

Wordsworth, William. "Preface to the Second Edition of *The Lyrical Ballads*." *Selected Poems and Prefaces of William Wordsworth*. Ed. Jack Stillinger. Boston: Houghton Mifflin Co., 1965. 445–68.

Wright, Willard Huntington. "The Great Detective Stories." *The Art of the Mystery Story*. Ed. Howard Haycraft. New York: Carroll & Graf, 1993. 33–70.

Index

– A –

Addams, Charles, 9
Age of Reason, 21, 22
"A" Is for Alibi (Grafton), 61
Alan Parsons Project, 9
American International Pictures, 114
American Renaissance (Mathiessen), 98
"Amorous Bondage: Poe, Ladies, and
    Slaves" (Dayan), 98
"Annabel Lee" (Poe), 72, 104
Apollonian influence, 30, 48
Apt Pupil (King), 105
Art Nouveau, 9
atavism, 42, 50–53
Atreus, 27
Auden, W. H.: 35, 42; "The Guilty
    Vicarage," 23, 31
audience, 2, 5, 19–21, 32, 34–35,
    38–39, 96–97;
    adolescent, 19, 20, 21, 34

– B –

Bacon, Francis, 38
"The Balloon Hoax" (Poe), 94
Barker, Clive, 93
Beaudelaire, 1, 68
Beckford, William: *Vathek*, 13, 15
"Berenice" (Poe), 2, 13, 15, 16, 20, 30,
    60, 69
The Bible, 3
The Big Sleep, 60
"The Birthmark" (Hawthorne), 49
Bitter Medicine (Paretsky), 59, 61, 63, 64
"The Black Cat" (Poe), 15–16, 19, 21, 23,
    24, 42, 58, 64, 73–74, 100, 113, 116
Black Sunday (Harris), 83
"Bloodstains" (Oates), 67–68
The Body (King), 104
Bonaparte, Marie: *The Life and
    Works of Edgar Allan Poe*, 20

Borges, Jorge Luis, 9
Borgo, Susan, 88
Bosch, Hieronymus: "The Garden
    of Earthly Delights," 122
Brite, Poppy Z., 66–67
Byron, Lord George, 13
Byronic hero, 13, 18, 32

– C –

"Calculus of Probabilities," 26
Caputi, Jane, 90
Carrie (King), 103
Carroll, Noël, 14, 18
"The Cask of Amontillado" (Poe),
    15–16, 70, 72, 106, 126
The Castle of Otranto (Walpole),
    13–14, 37, 66
Christie, Agatha: 36, 57; *The Murder
    of Roger Ackroyd*, 35, 41
clocks, 16, 105–6, 113
Clover, Carol, 39, 66
Corman, Roger, 8, 114–19, 129
The Cosmos (von Humboldt), 99
Crane, Jonathan Lake, 38
Crime and Punishment (Dostoevsky),
    19, 82

– D –

Danse Macabre (King), 6
The Dark Half (King), 107–08
Darwin, Charles, 40
Darwinism, 50–51, 53
Dayan, Joan: 17; "Amorous
    Bondage: Poe, Ladies, and
    Slaves," 98
The Dead Zone (King), 95
"death warrant," 36–37, 119
Debussy, Claude, 9
Demme, Jonathan, 114

"Descent into the Maelstrom"
(Poe), 15
detection: and horror, 29–44, 77–91;
feminized, 57–75; in film,
113–29; Victorian, 45–55
Dick, Philip K., 127
Dickerson, Mary Jane, 99
Dickinson, Emily, 74
Dionysian influence, 30, 48
"Dolan's Cadillac" (King), 106
Dolores Claiborne (King), 66, 95–96,
105, 107
Donne, John, 80
doppelgänger, 18
Dostoevsky, Fyodor: 68, 89; *Crime
and Punishment*, 19, 82; *Notes
from Underground*, 23
Dove, George, 36–37, 119
Doyle, Arthur Conan: 35, 48, 50–53,
107; *The Hound of the
Baskervilles*, 7, 26, 31, 33, 40–41,
48–49, 51–53, 54–55, 58, 121;
A Scandal in Bohemia, 45–46;
A Study in Scarlet, 35, 45
Dracula (Stoker), 62, 66
"The Dungeon" (Oates), 68–69

– E –

Edmundson, Mark: *Nightmare on
Main Street*, 43, 95
Eighty Seventh Precinct series
(McBain), 61, 107
"Eleanora" (Poe), 16, 68
Eliot, T. S., 1, 20–21
Elmer, Jonathan, 96
Enlightenment, 28, 53
Eureka: A Prose Poem (Poe), 99
Evans, Walter: "Monster Movies: A
Sexual Theory," 20
evolution, 40, 51
Expansionism, 98

– F –

"The Fall of the House of Usher"
(Poe), 8, 13, 15–17, 29, 36, 43, 60, 105
Faulkner, William, 99
"A Fever," 80
feminism, 42, 57–59, 69, 72, 74, 96,
115–16
Fielder, Leslie, 20, 98
"Final Girl," 39, 66
The Fine Art of Murder, 119
formula for detection, 36–37
Freud, Sigmund, 41
films: *Alien*, 66; *Apolcalypse Now*, 129;
Blade Runner, 4, 8, 121, 125–28;
The Blob, 41; *Chinatown*, 4, 8, 37,
119–21; *The Dead Zone*, 109–11;
Friday the 13th, 34, 38; *Halloween*,
34, 66; *Hearts of Darkness*, 129;
House of Usher, 115, 117; *Kiss
the Girls*, 66, 121; *L. A. Confidential*,
121; *The Making of Titanic*, 129; *The
Maltese Falcon*, 119; *Manhunter*, 121;
Masque of the Red Death, 116, 118–
19; *Nightmare on Elm Street*, 34;
Pit and the Pendulum, 116–18;
Psycho, 8; *Rear Window*, 8; *Texas
Chainsaw Massacre*, 38; *Seven*, 4, 8,
121–25, 127; *The Silence of the
Lambs*, 39, 78, 114; *The Thing*, 41;
Tightrope, 121; *Tomb of Ligeia*,
115, 117; *Vertigo*, 8
film noir, 4, 6, 113–29
Fisher, Benjamin Franklin: "The
Residual Gothic Impulse: 1824–
1873" (Fisher), 13–14
Five Bells and Bladebone (Grimes), 37
Fowler, Christopher: "The Master
Builder," 66
Frank, Frederick, 12–13
Frankenstein (Shelley), 32, 37, 88–91

– G –

"G" Is for Gumshoe (Grafton), 59,
61–64

"The Garden of Earthly Delights"
(Bosch), 122

Gaudy Night (Sayers), 57

gender, 21, 40, 57–75, 77, 78, 84–91, 97

genetic code for detection, 36–37

Gerald's Game (King), 66, 95–96, 105,
108

"The Golden Horseshoe," 37

Golden Age of Detection, 4

"Goldilocks and the Three Bears," 3–4

Grafton, Sue: 43, 65; *"A" Is for Alibi*,
59; *"G" Is for Gumshoe*, 59, 61–64;
"I" Is for Innocent, 62;
"J" Is for Judgment, 59

Grimes, Martha: *Five Bells and
Bladebone*, 37

Grisham, John, 99

Griswold, Rufus, 1

"The Guilty Vicarage" (Auden), 23, 31

– H –

Halberstam, Judith: 40; *Skin Shows*,
86–87, 90

Hamlet (Shakespeare), 3

Hammett, Dashiell: 107; *The Maltese
Falcon*, 60

Harris, Thomas: 7, 32; *Black Sunday*,
83; *Red Dragon*, 83; *The Silence
of the Lambs*, 7, 32, 34, 39–40, 66,
77–91

Haunted: Tales of the Grotesque
(Oates), 70

Hawthorne, Nathaniel: 2, 32, 37,
98–99; "The Birthmark," 49

Hemingway, Ernest, 60, 99

Hill Street Blues, 82

Hitchcock, Alfred, 8

Homicide, 82

"Hop-Frog" (Poe), 70, 118

horror: and detection, 29–44, 77–91;
feminized, 57–75; in film, 113–29;
Victorian, 47–57

The Hound of the Baskervilles (Doyle),
7, 26, 31, 33, 40, 41, 45, 48, 51,
54–55, 58, 121

Housewright, David: *Penance*, 37

Humboldt, Heinrich Alexander Baron
von: *The Cosmos*, 99

Huston, John, 119

– I –

"I" Is for Innocent (Grafton), 62

"The Imp of the Perverse" (Poe), 14, 15,
16, 22–23, 25, 53

IT (King), 4, 43, 99, 105

– J –

"J" Is for Judgment (Grafton), 59

"Judge Lynch," 21

– K –

Kafka, Franz: 9, 68

Keats, John, 12

Kent, Brian, 97

King, Stephen: 7, 31, 43, 93–111, 118; *Apt
Pupil*, 105; *The Body*, 104; *Carrie*, 103;
Danse Macabre, 6; *The Dark Half*,
107–8; *The Dead Zone*, 95; "Dolan's
Cadillac," 106; *Dolores Claiborne*, 66,
95–96, 105, 107; *Gerald's Game*, 66,
95–96, 105, 108; *IT*, 4, 43, 99, 105;
Needful Things, 107; *Nightmares and
Dreamscapes*, 106; *Pet Sematary*, 95,
99, 105; *Rose Madder*, 66, 95–96;
The Shawshank Redemption, 107;
The Shining, 14, 32, 93, 95, 100–6, 108;
The Stand, 95; "Why We Crave Horror
Movies," 18

Koja, Kathie, 66–67

– L –

Laplace, Pierre Simon Marquis de, 99
"Later Victorian Ghost Stories: The
    Literature of Belief" (Sheridan), 48
layered narrative, 54
Leverenz, David: "Poe and Gentry
    Virginia," 98
Lewis, Matthew: 18, 69; *The Monk*, 15
"Ligeia" (Poe), 8, 13, 15, 16, 30, 60, 64,
    113, 128
Longfellow, Henry Wadsworth, 1
The Life and Works of Edgar Allan Poe
    (Bonaparte), 20

– M –

MacDonald, John D., 107
Magistrale, Tony, 99
The Maltese Falcon (Hammett), 60
"The Man of the Crowd" (Poe), 14, 23–24
"The Masque of the Red Death" (Poe), 13,
    93, 99, 101, 105, 108, 113–14, 116
"The Master Builder" (Fowler), 66
Masse, Michelle A., 69
Mathiessen, F. O.: 97; *American
    Renaissance*, 98
McBain, Ed: 82; Eighty-Seventh
    Precinct series, 61, 107
Melville, Herman, 2, 98
"Metzengerstein" (Poe), 13
Modernism, 1
The Monk (Lewis), 15
"Monster Movies: A Sexual Theory"
    (Evans), 20
"Morella" (Poe), 13, 15, 16, 17, 58
Morgan, Robin, 90
"The Murders in the Rue Morgue"
    (Poe), 2, 22, 24–26, 30, 36, 65, 85
The Murder of Roger Ackroyd
    (Christie), 35, 41
"The Mystery of Marie Roget"
    (Poe), 26, 94

– N –

NYPD Blue, 82
Nabokov, Vladimir, 47
Needful Things (King), 107
Neoclassicism, 11, 12, 21
New England, 96, 98
Nicholson, Jack, 32
Nietzsche, Friedrich, 30
Nightmare on Main Street
    (Edmundson), 43, 95
Nightmares and Dreamscapes
    (King), 106
Notes from Underground
    (Dostoevsky), 23

– O –

Oates, Joyce Carol: 67–75;
    "Bloodstains," 67–68; "The
    Dungeon," 68–69; *Haunted:
    Tales of the Grotesque*, 70; "The
    Premonition," 70–72; "Where
    Are You Going, Where Have You
    Been?," 69; "The White Cat,"
    73–74
Oedipus Rex, 2–3

– P –

Panek, Leroy Lad, 26
Paretsky, Sara: 40, 65, 78; *Bitter
    Medicine*, 59, 61, 63, 64
Parker, Robert B., 60
Paul, Robert S., 21
Penance (Housewright), 37
Pet Sematary (King), 95, 99, 105
Pinakidia (Poe), 13
"The Philosophy of Composition"
    (Poe) 17, 25, 37, 85, 115, 128–29
phrenology, 22–23
"The Pit and the Pendulum" (Poe)
    15, 30, 38–39, 86, 105

place, 14–16, 25–26, 37–38, 46–48, 63–
64, 68, 71–72, 85–86, 90, 101–2, 105
"Poe and Gentry Virginia" (Leverenz),
98
Poe, Edgar Allan: "close
circumscription of space," 25, 37,
85; "Annabel Lee," 72, 104; "The
Balloon Hoax," 94; "Berenice," 2,
13, 15, 16, 20, 30, 60, 69; "The Black
Cat," 15–16, 19, 21, 23, 24, 42, 58, 64,
73–74, 100, 113, 116; "The Cask
of Amontillado," 15–16, 70, 72, 106,
126; "Descent into the Maelstrom,"
15; "Eleanora," 16, 68; *Eureka: A
Prose Poem*, 101; "The Fall of the
House of Usher," 8, 13, 15–17, 29, 36,
43, 60, 105; "Hop-Frog," 70, 118;
"The Imp of the Perverse," 14, 15, 16,
53; "Ligeia," 8, 13, 15, 16, 30, 60, 64,
113, 128; "The Man of the Crowd," 14,
23–24; "The Masque of the Red
Death," 13, 15, 93, 99, 101, 105, 108, 113,
114, 116; "Metzengerstein," 13;
"Morella," 13, 15, 16, 17, 58;
"The Murders in the Rue Morgue,"
2, 22, 24–26, 30, 36, 65, 85;
"The Mystery of Marie Roget," 26,
94; *Pinakidia*, 13; "The Philosophy
of Composition," 17, 25, 37, 85, 115,
128–29; "The Pit and the Pendulum"
15, 30, 38–39, 86, 105; "The Purloined
Letter," 16, 18, 26–28, 30, 33, 45, 65,
79, 82, 85; "The Poetic Principle,"
11–12; "The Premature Burial," 13;
"The Raven," 1, 85, 108–11, 129; "The
Tell–Tale Heart," 2, 14, 15, 16, 17, 19, 21,
24, 29, 36, 38, 42, 58, 64, 70, 72, 100,
113, 116, 126; "Thou Art the Man," 13;
"Ulalume," 85; "William Wilson," 16,
18–20, 27, 29, 48, 108, 126
"The Poetic Principle" (Poe), 11–12
Polanski, Roman, 121
police procedural, 82

*Preface to the Second Edition of The
Lyrical Ballads* (Wordsworth), 12–13
"The Premature Burial" (Poe), 13
"The Premonition" (Oates), 70–72
Price, Vincent, 114, 117, 118
"The Purloined Letter" (Poe), 16, 18,
26–28, 30, 33, 45, 65, 79, 82, 85

– R –
Radcliffe, Ann, 62
Rajan, Gita, 72
"The Raven" (Poe), 1, 85, 108–11, 129
Red Dragon (Harris), 83
Reesman, Jeanne Campbell, 99
"The Residual Gothic Impulse: 1824–
1873" (Fisher), 13–14
Rice, Ann, 66–67
Romanticism, 11–12, 28, 50
Rose Madder (King), 66, 95–96

– S –
Salvi, John, 29
Sayers, Dorothy L.: *Gaudy Night*, 57
A Scandal in Bohemia (Doyle), 45–46
science, 48–49, 55, 88, 94
science fiction, 125
Scott, Ridley, 125
sensory details, 113–14
Shakespeare, William: 2; *Hamlet*, 3;
The Tempest, 13, 99
The Shawshank Redemption (King),
107
Shelley, Mary: 130; *Frankenstein*, 32, 37,
88–90
Sheridan, Daniel: "Later Victorian
Ghost Stories: The Literature of
Belief," 48
The Shining (King), 14, 32, 93, 95,
100–6, 108
The Silence of the Lambs (Harris), 7,
32, 34, 39–40, 66, 77–91

Simmons, Dan, 91
"The Simpsons," 1
Skin Shows (Halberstam), 86–87, 90
Soukup, Barbara, 71
The Stand (King), 95
Stasio, Marilyn, 59
Steele, Danielle, 99
Stevenson, Robert Louis: 36, 53; *The Strange Case of Dr. Jekyll and Mr. Hyde*, 7, 19, 40, 45–52, 55, 88–90
Stoker, Bram: 69; *Dracula*, 62, 66
The Strange Case of Dr. Jekyll and Mr. Hyde (Stevenson), 7, 19, 40, 45–52, 55, 88–90
A Study in Scarlet (Doyle), 35, 45
Symbolist Movement, 1

– T –
television: *Hill Street Blues*, 82; *Homicide*, 82; *NYPD Blue*, 82; "The Simpsons," 1
"The Tell-Tale Heart" (Poe), 2, 14–17, 19, 21, 24, 29, 36, 38, 42, 58, 64, 70, 72, 100, 113, 116, 126
Telotte, J. P., 126
The Tempest (Shakespeare), 13, 99
Tessier, Thomas, 96
Thornton, Steven, 118
"Thou Art the Man" (Poe), 13
Thyestes, 27
time, 16, 105–06, 114
Transcendentalism, 98
"Twenty Rules for Writing Detective Stories" (Van Dine), 60
Twitchell, James B., 14

– U –
"Ulalume" (Poe), 85

– V –
Van Dine, S. S., 36; "Twenty Rules for Writing Detective Stories," 60
Van Gogh, Vincent, 9
vampire lore, 13, 43
Vathek (Beckford), 13, 15

– W –
Walpole, Horace: *The Castle of Otranto*, 13–14, 37, 66
Weber, Jean-Paul, 16
"Where Are You Going, Where Have You Been?" (Oates), 69
"The White Cat" (Oates), 73–74
"Who Cares Who Killed Roger Ackroyd" (Wilson, Edmund), 2
"Why We Crave Horror Movies" (King), 18
Williams, Linda, 57
Williams, William Carlos, 99
"William Wilson" (Poe), 16, 18–20, 27, 29, 48, 108, 126
Wilson, Edmund: "Who Cares Who Killed Roger Ackroyd," 2
Wilson, Gahan, 9
Wood, Robin, 8, 32
Wordsworth, William: *Preface to the Second Edition of The Lyrical Ballads*, 12–13